MAGNIFICENT BEASTS
A COLOURING BOOK QUEST

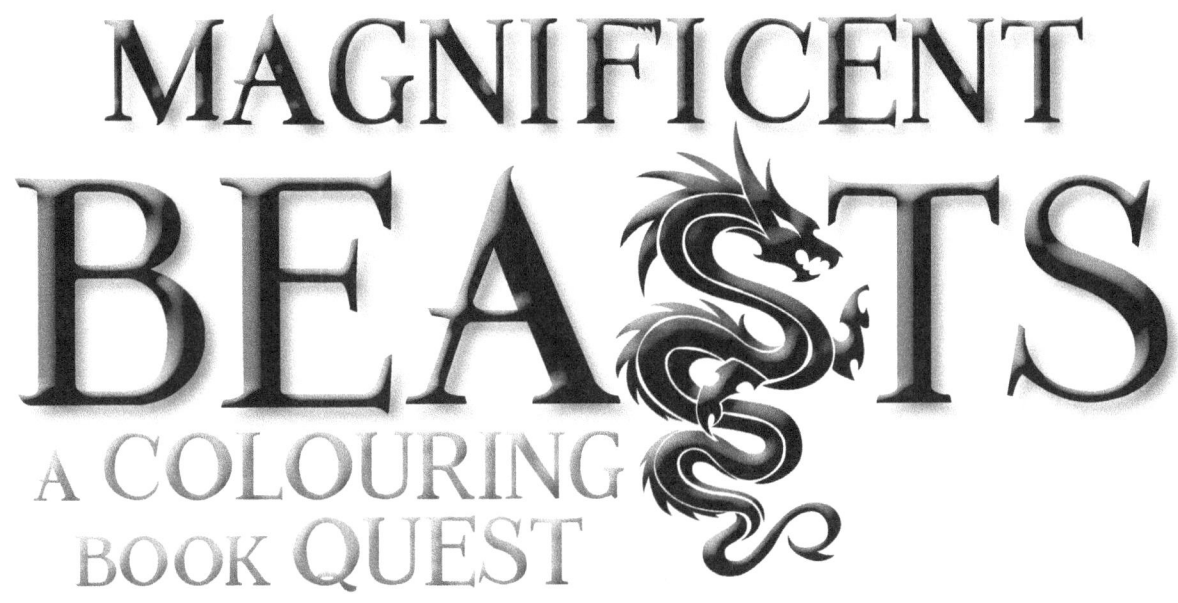

First published in the United Kingdom in 2017 by
Bell & Mackenzie Publishing Limited

Copyright © Bell & Mackenzie Publishing Limited 2017

All rights reserved. This book or any portion thereof may not be reproduced or used
in any manner whatsoever without the express written permission of the publisher.

ISBN: 978-1-912155-19-4

Created by Christina Rose

Contributors: Under licence from Shutterstock

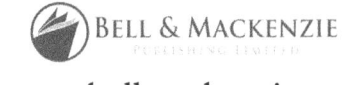

BELL & MACKENZIE
PUBLISHING LIMITED

www.bellmackenzie.com

A phoenix is an ancient beast bird which symbolises regeneration and re-birth. Rising from the ashes, Greek mythology associates the Phoenix with the sun.

The story of the phoenix has been retold countless times over the centuries. Living for up to 1400 years at a time, some believe the phoenix dies in a show of flames and combustion whilst there are others who tell tales of the legendary bird dying and simply decomposing before being born again.

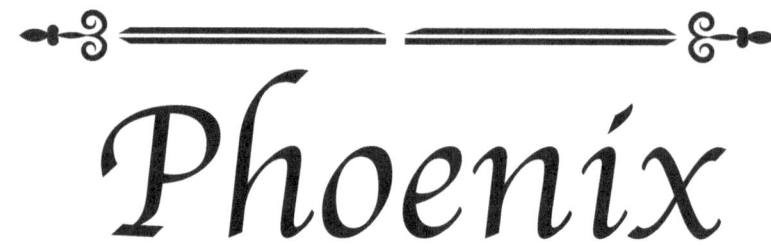

Phoenix

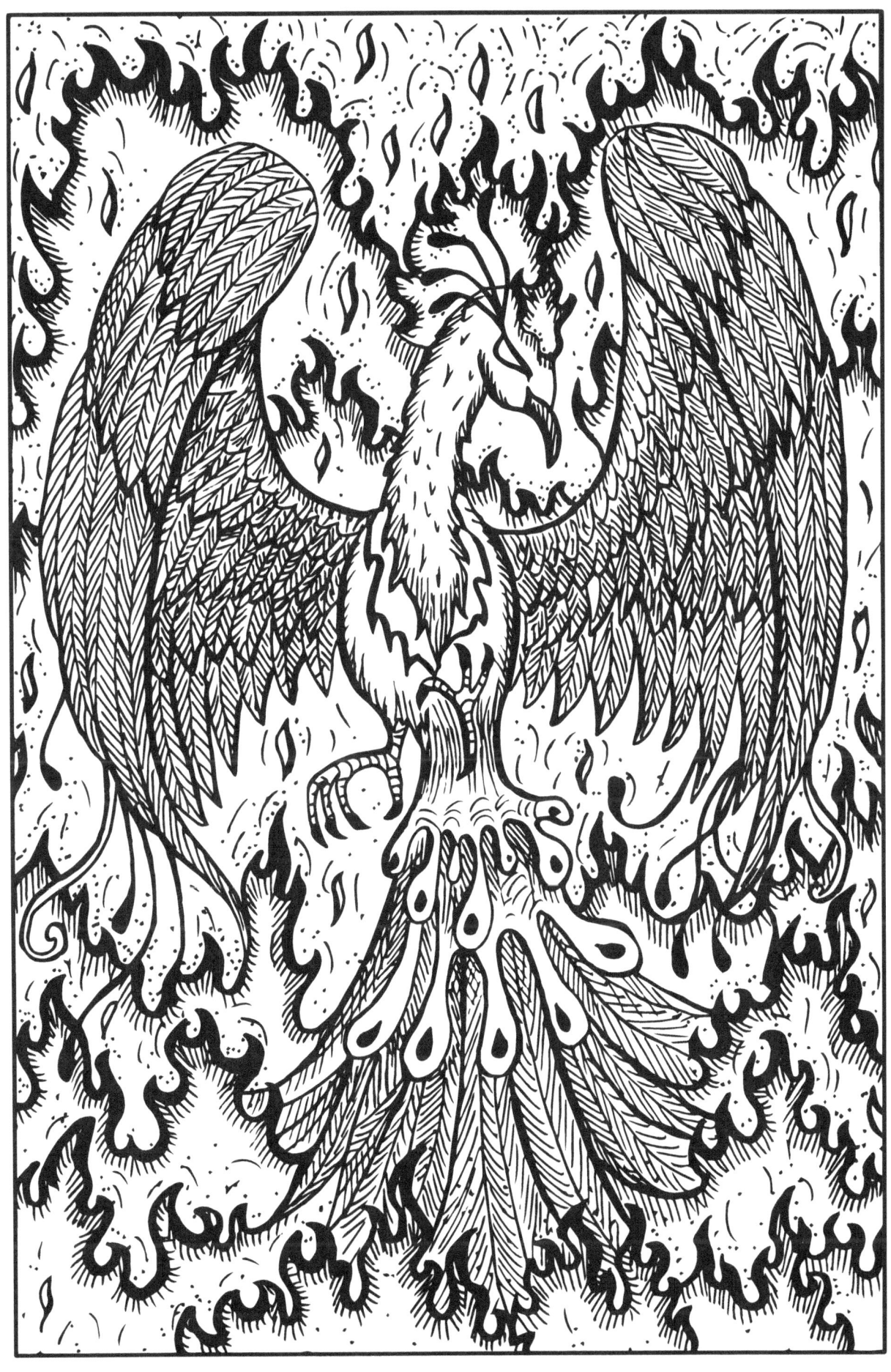

European legend tells of this king of serpents that is said to have the power to cause death with a single glance. It is believed to be venomous, it leaves a wide trail of deadly venom in its wake with its gaze being equally lethal.

It can sometimes be tracked as it leaves surrounding shrubs scorched by its presence. It's thought Basilisk provided inspiration for some of the modern folklore surrounding the King Cobra.

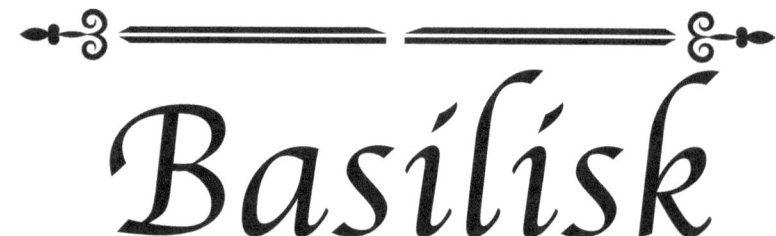

Basilisk

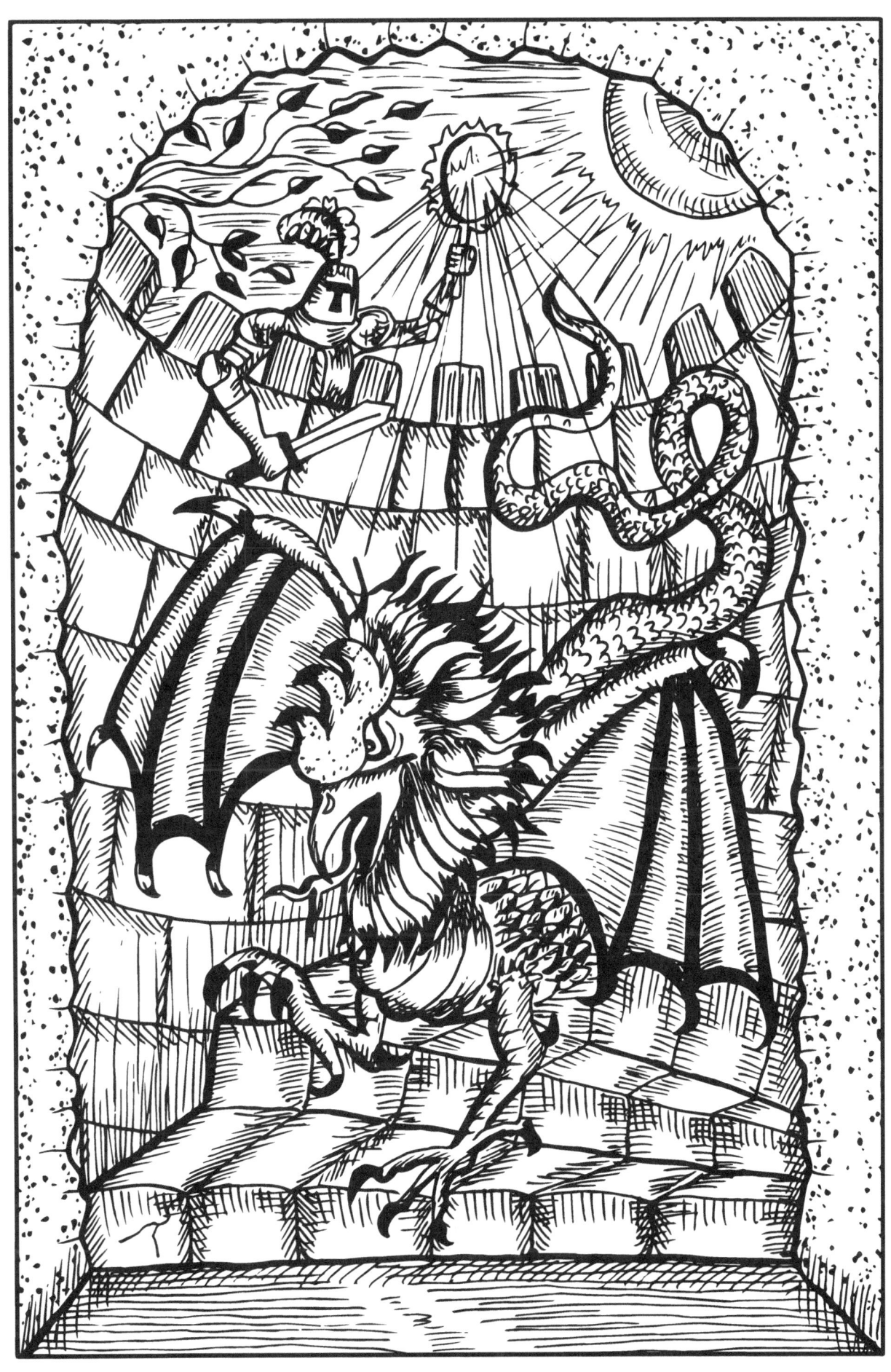

Dating from 631 – 641 AD, French legend sprang up around the chancellor of the Merovingian king Clotaire II who was made bishop of Rouen.

Arriving in Rouen the bishop discovered a monster called Gargouille. La Gargouille is said to be a dragon with batlike wings and the ability to breathe fire from its mouth. The bishop goes on to capture the beast by subduing it with his crucifix. The creature is then burned but it's head and neck could not be destroyed as these were already tempered by its own fire breath.

The head of La Gargouille was then mounted on the walls of a newly built church to scare off evil spirits, which is why you will find stone Gargoyle heads mounted on ancient architecture all over the world.

Gargoyle

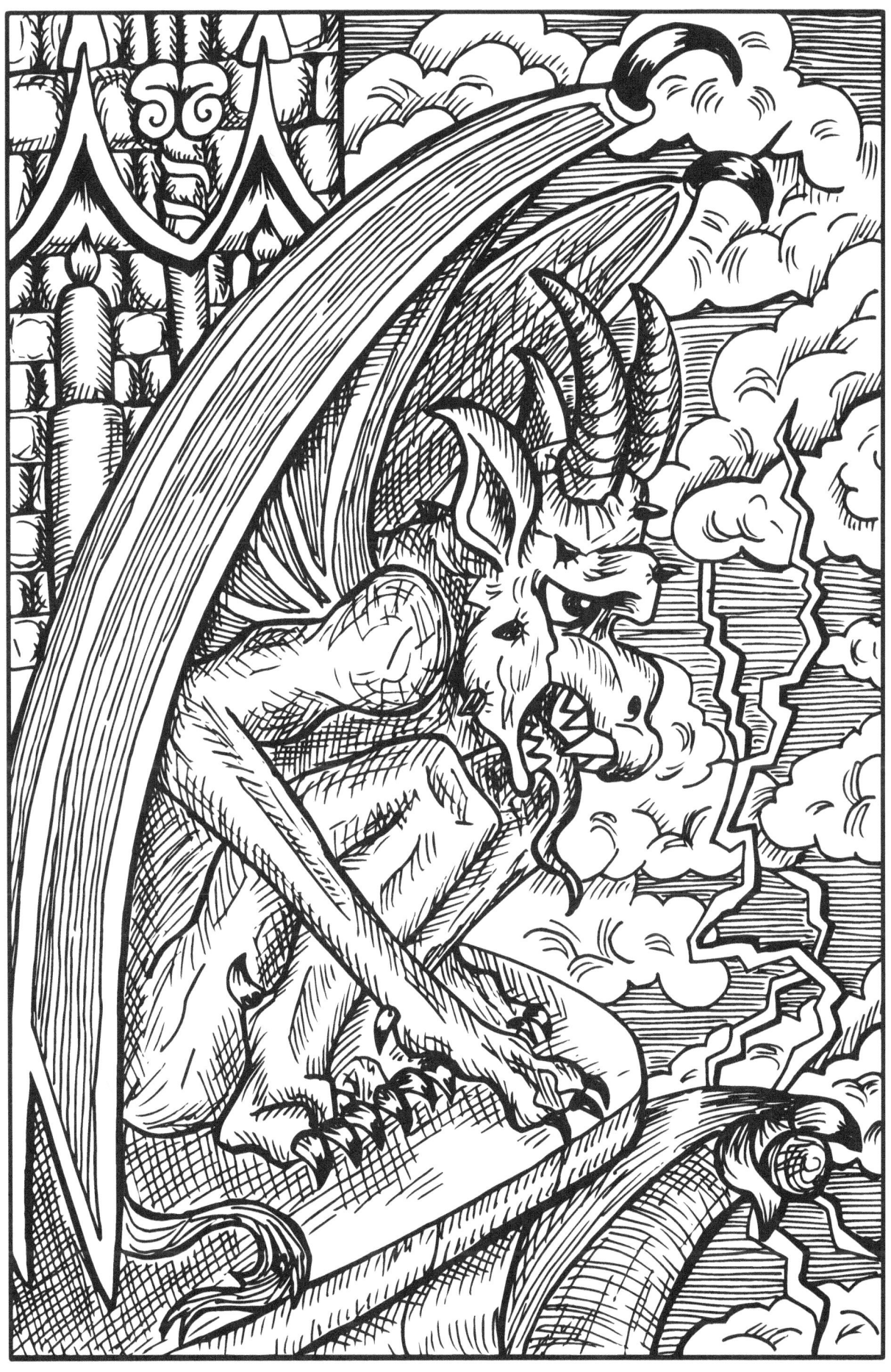

In Greek mythology a harpy is a female beast in the form of a bird with a human face. Believed to be 'wind' spirits, Harpies steal food from their victims while they carry evildoers to the Greek Goddesses of vengeance Erinyes to be tortured.

In Canto XIII of his Inferno, Dante Alighieri describes the tortured wood infested with harpies, where the suicides have their punishment in the seventh ring of Hell. Although originally depicted as ugly they were immortalized in Roman pottery as beautiful women with wings.

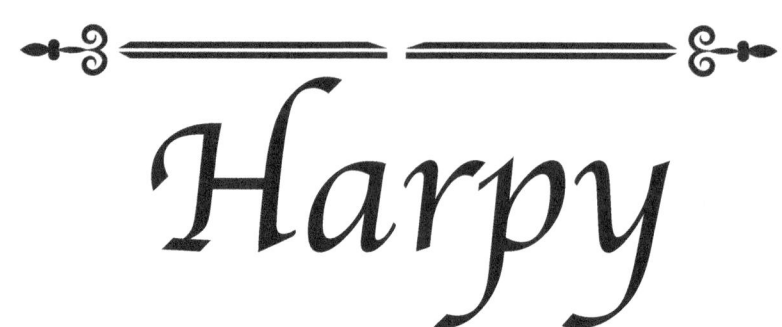

Harpy

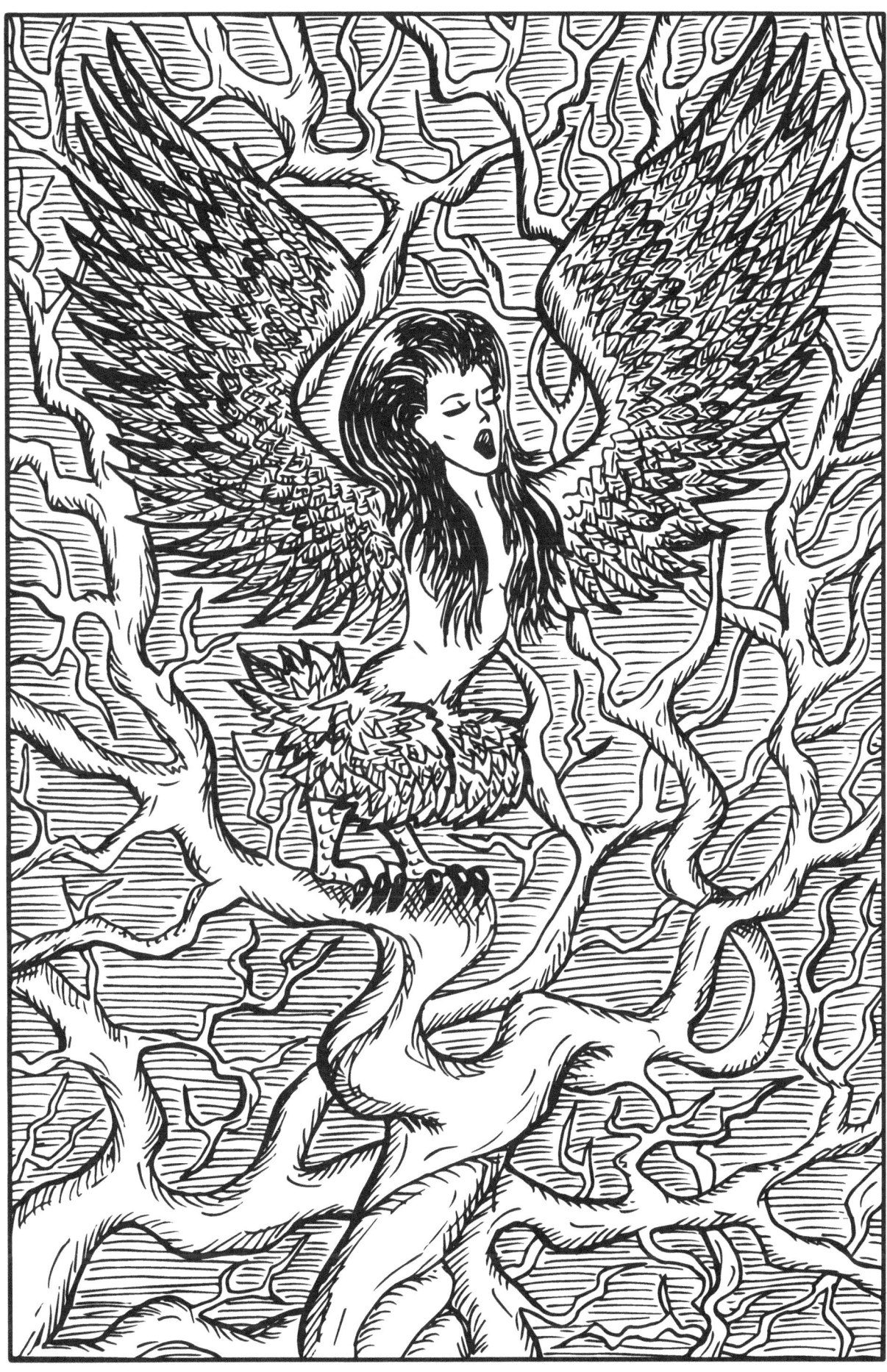

*O*riginally born from a cloud, the Centaurs were said to have inhabited the region of Magnesia and Mount Pelion in Thessaly, the Foloi oak forest in Elis, and the Malean peninsula in southern Laconia.

Another tribe of centaurs, which were horned, inhabited Cyprus and were thought to have been born of the Greek God Zeus, who, in frustration after Aphrodite had rebuked him, spilled his seed on the ground of Cyprus.

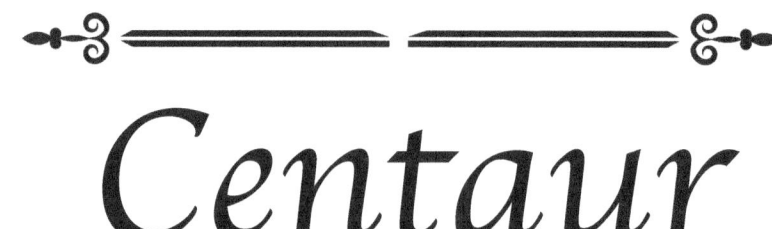

Centaur

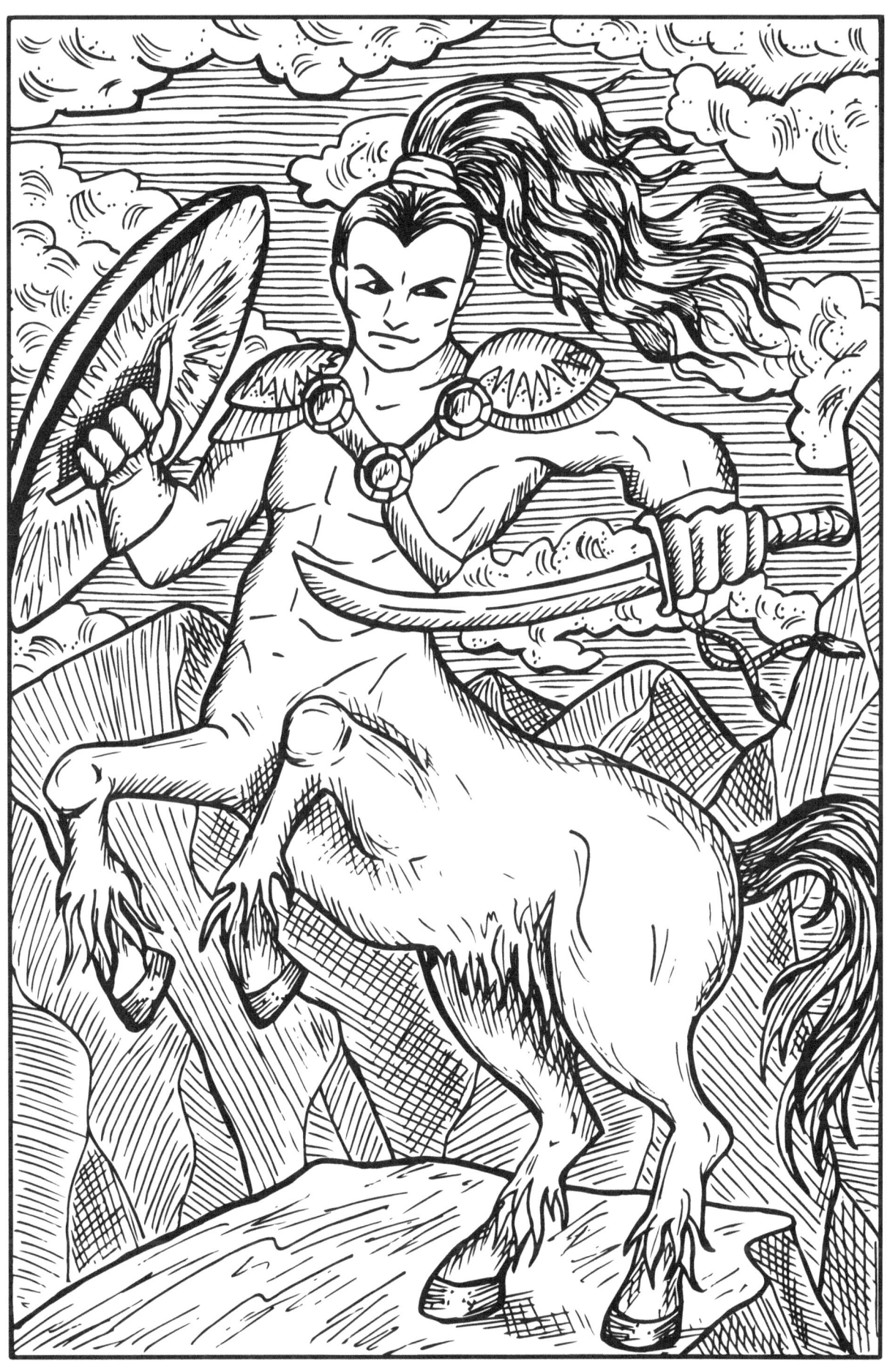

Pegasus is one of the most recognisable creatures in Greek mythology. A great winged stallion, Pegasus is often depicted as pure white in colour or with a golden mane. He was sired by Poseidon, in his role as horse-god, and foaled by the Gorgon Medusa.

Captured by the Greek hero Bellerophon, Pegasus allowed himself to be ridden in a great battle before Zeus transformed him into the constellation Pegasus and placed him up in the sky.

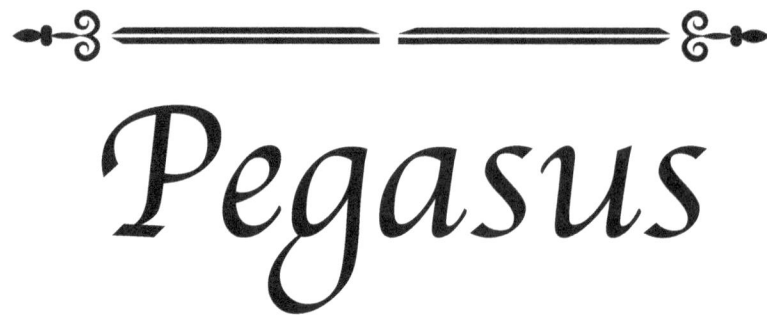

Pegasus

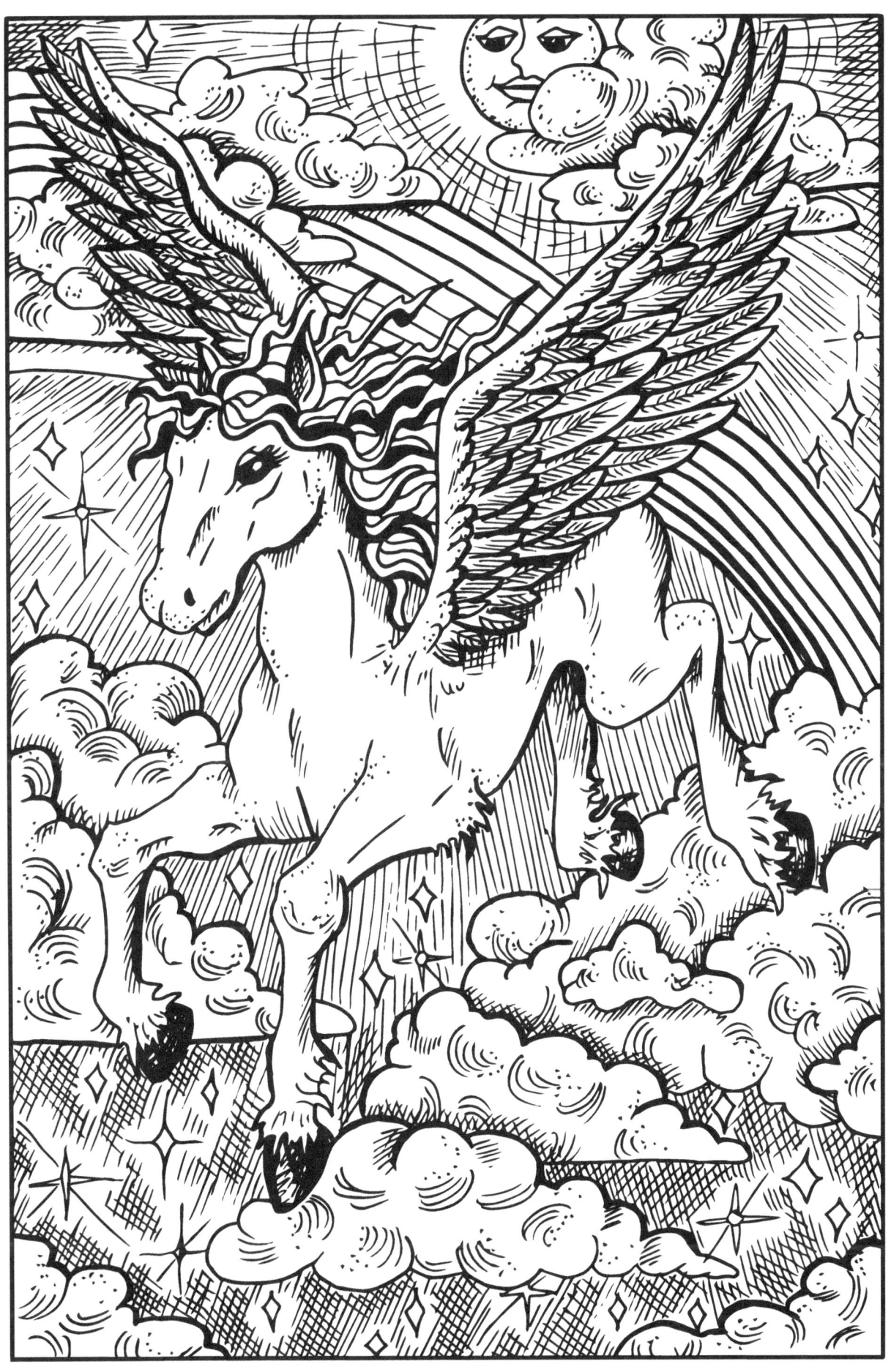

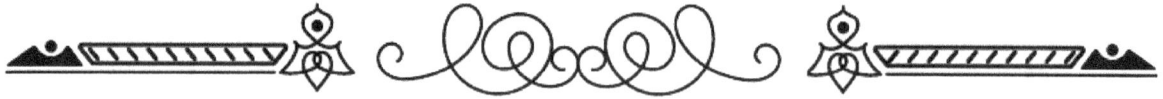

First referenced in the Old Testament of the bible: "God is praised for having made all things, including Leviathan" and in Isaiah 27:1 he is called the "tortuous serpent" who will be killed at the end of time.

In the Middle Ages Leviathan was used as an image of Satan, endangering God's creatures & creation by threatening it with upheaval in the waters of chaos.

Leviathan has become synonymous with any large sea monster or creature. It is a symbol of the monstrous and anarchic primordial world.

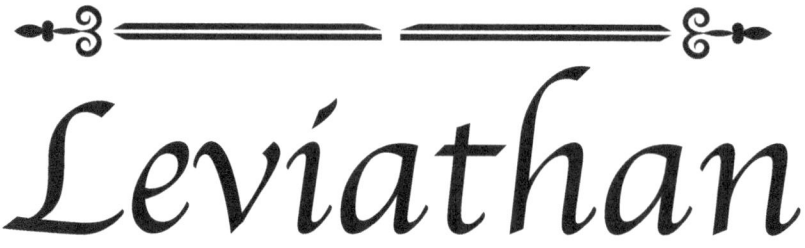

Leviathan

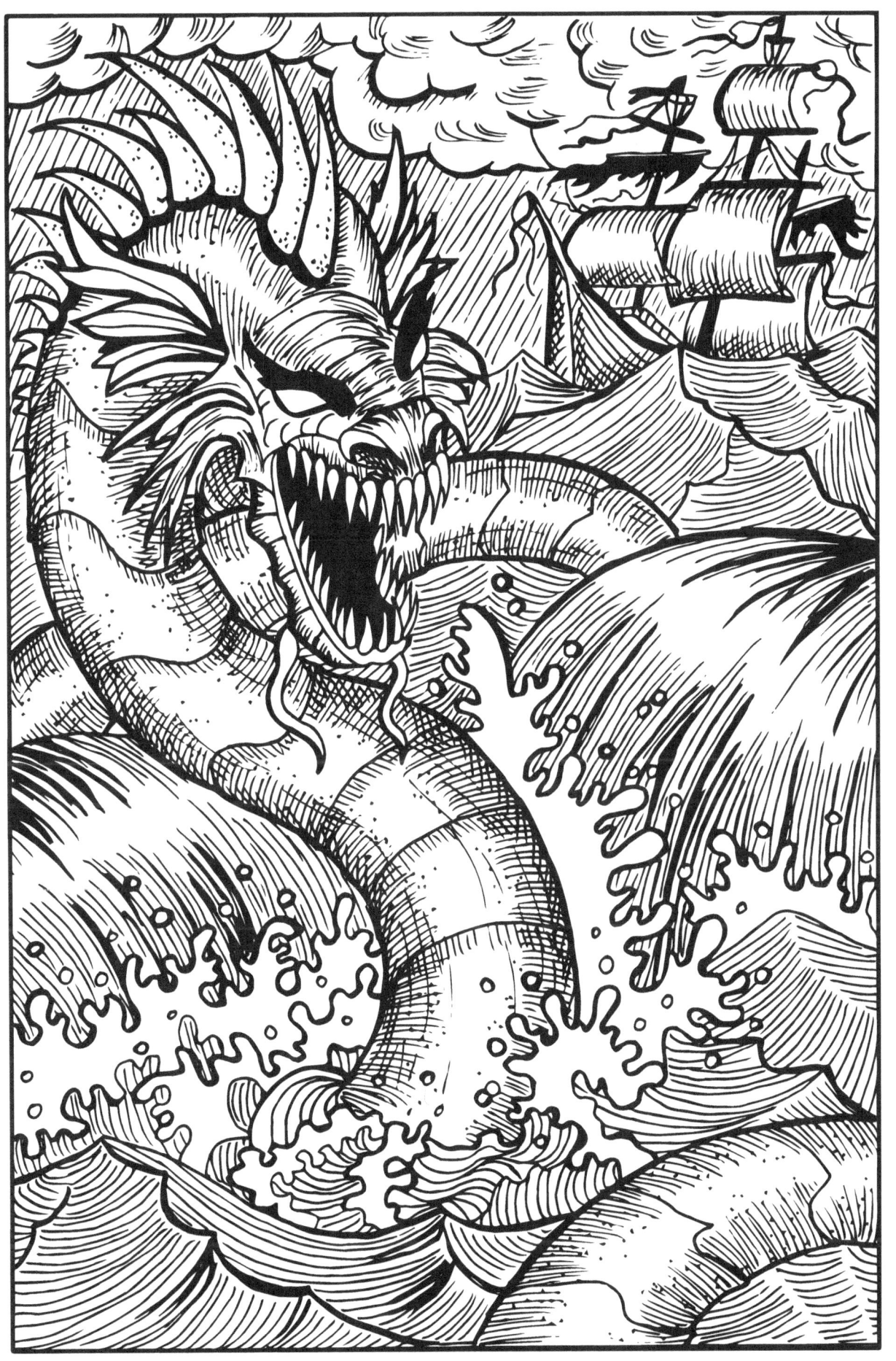

A Greek mythological character this man beast is the god of the wild. His concerns include shepherds and flocks, nature, mountain wilds as well as rustic music and performance. He finds companionship with the nymphs and he has the hindquarters, legs, and horns of a goat.

Pan is connected to the season of spring and thus has become a symbol of fertility. Sometimes depicted as a theatrical lover of the arts Pan has a more beastly side to his character. His angry temper is thought to inspire panic in lonely places.

Following an assault on Olympus, Pan claimed credit for the victory of the gods because he had frightened the attackers by instilling panic in the hearts of their enemies.

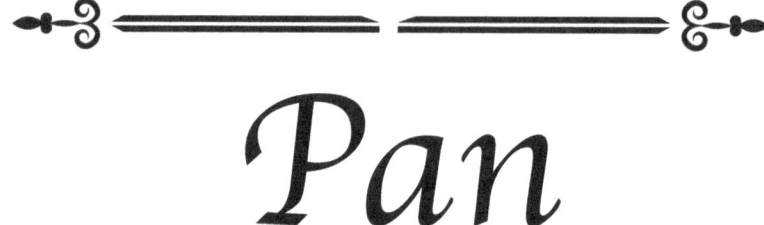

Pan

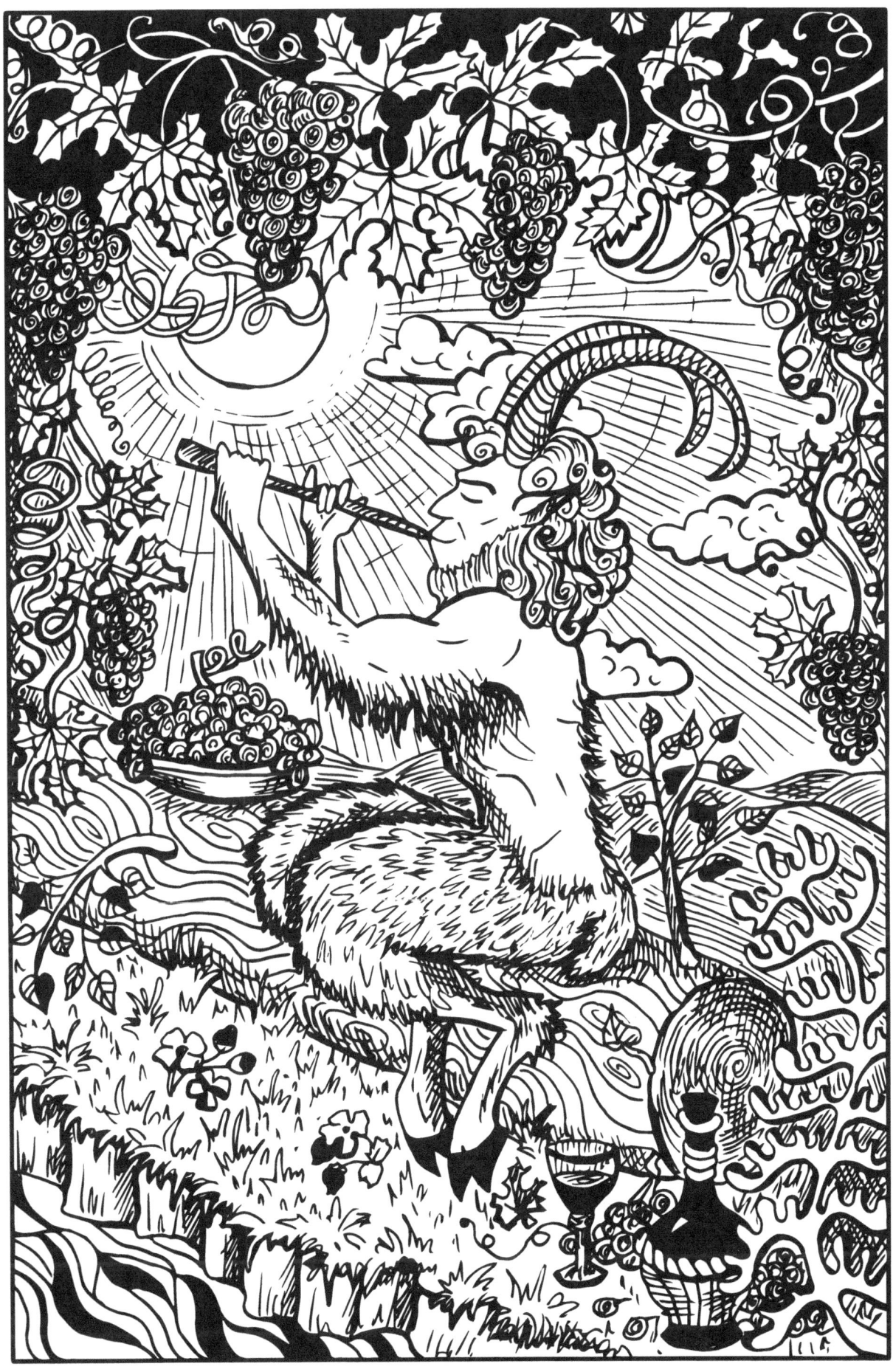

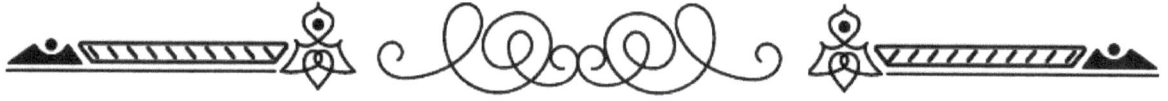

$\mathcal{A}$ demon is a malevolent, supernatural being widespread in religion, occultism, mythology and folklore.

Depicted in a variety of forms a demon is usually considered an unclean spirit, a fallen angel, or a spirit of unknown type that may cause demonic possession.

In some cultures it is believed that the power of a demon-beast as a spiritual entity can be controlled by a holy man and thus harnessed for good or evil human purposes.

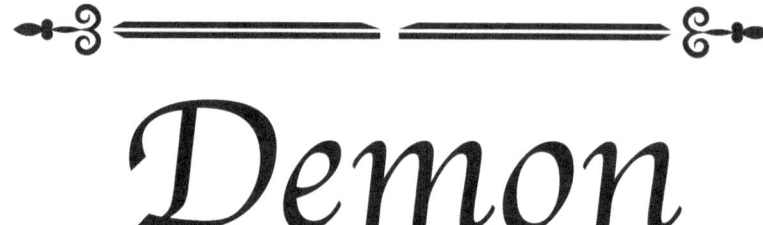

Demon

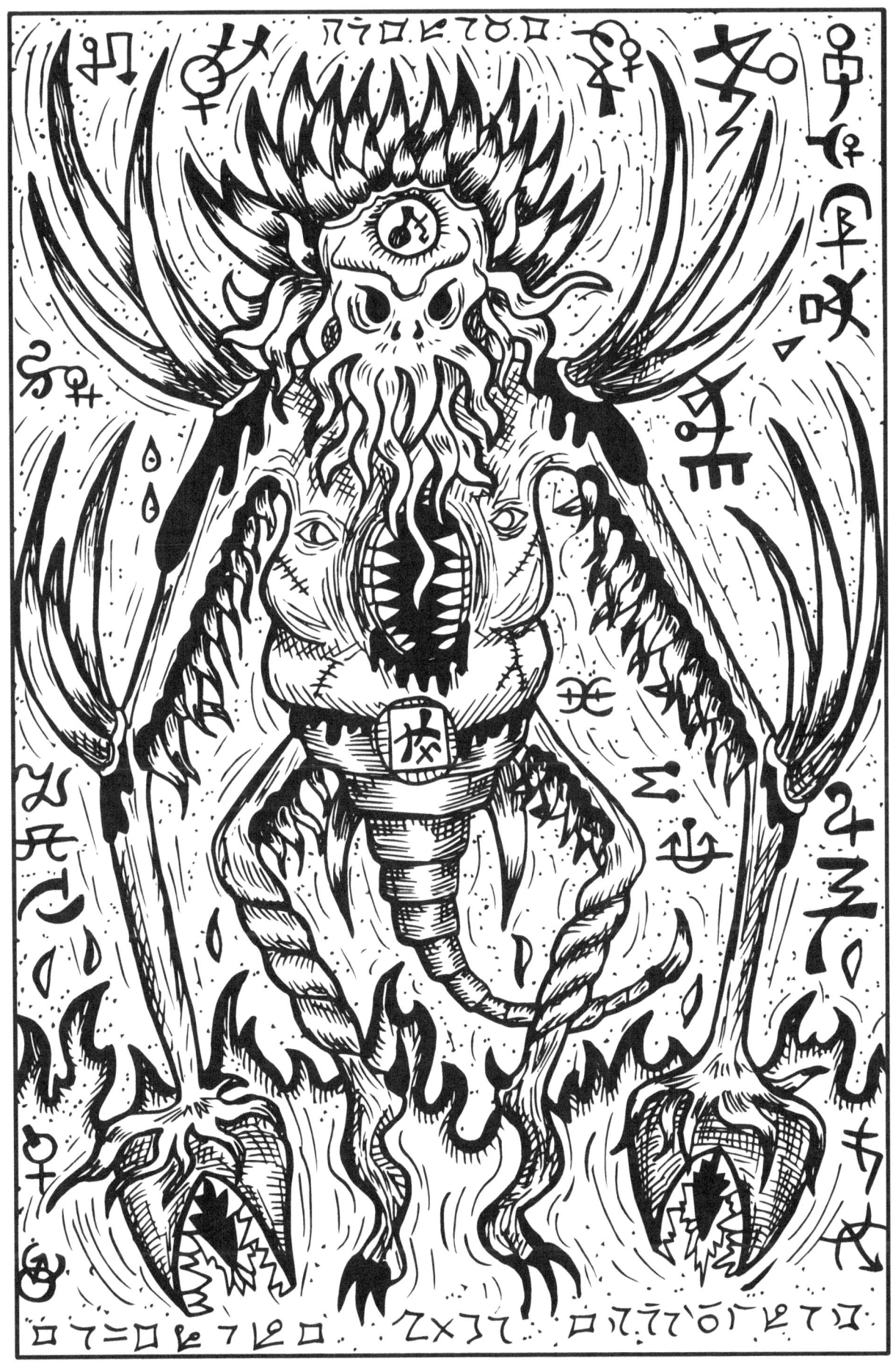

*T*he Griffon is a legendary creature with the body of a lion;
the head, wings and talons of an eagle. Also known as a griffin
or gryphon it is an especially powerful and majestic beast
considered to be the king of all creatures as it merges the king of
the air (the eagle) with the king of the land (the lion)

Griffins are known for guarding treasure and priceless
possessions and are associated with gold. It is said griffins lay
eggs in burrows that contain gold nuggets.

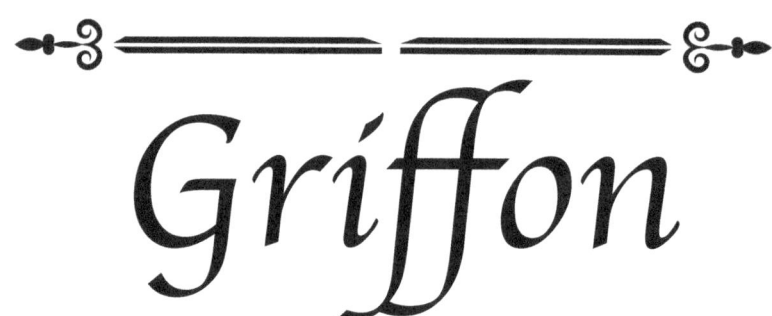

Griffon

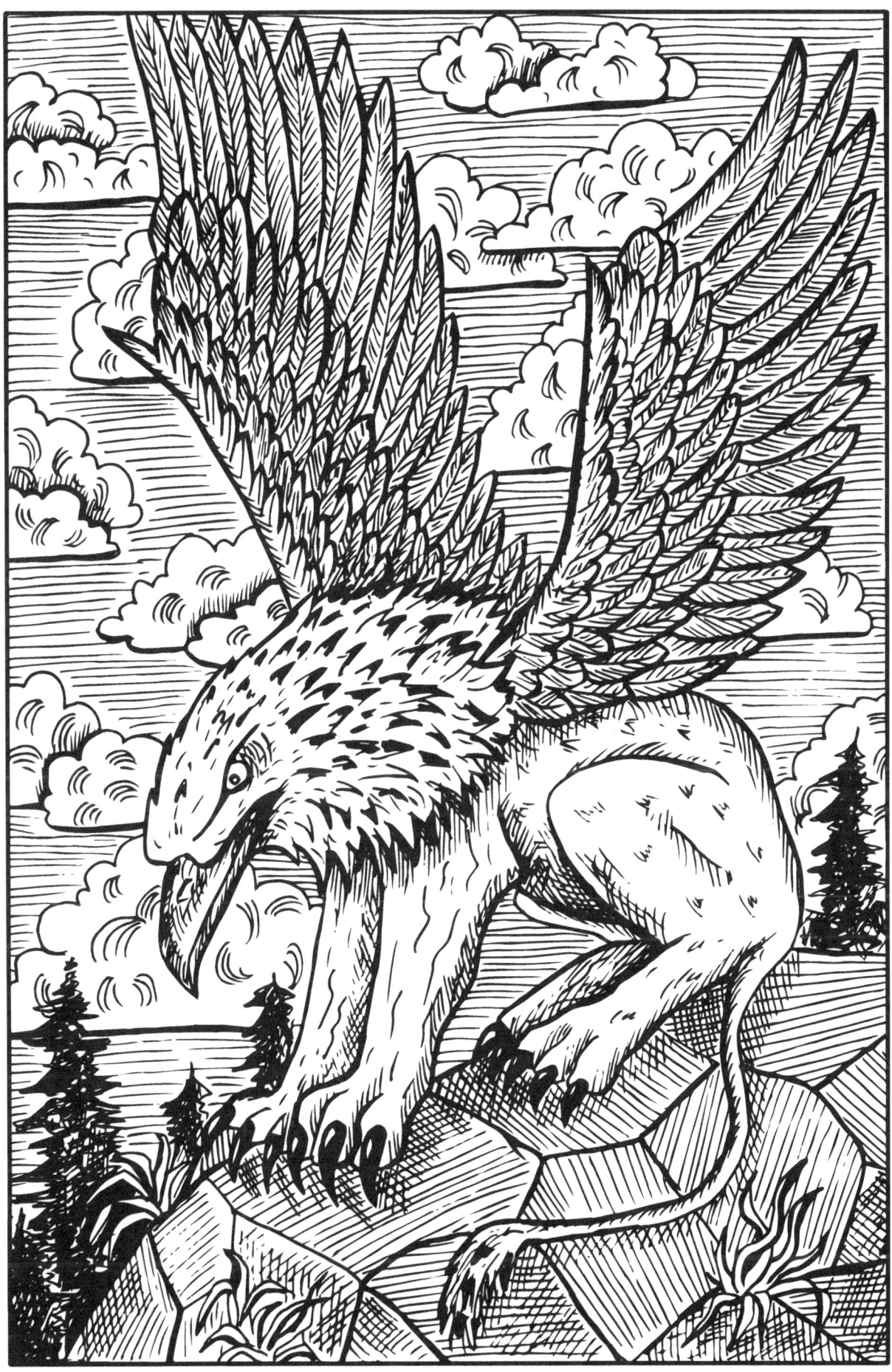

Often called the "hound of Hades", Cerbeus is a monstrous multi-headed dog that guards the gates of the underworld to prevent the dead from leaving.

Cerberus is usually described as having three heads and a serpent for a tail. The father of Cerbeus was the multi snake-headed Typhon, and he is also the brother of three other multi-headed monsters, Lernaean Hydra and Chimera.

Cerbeus was thought to have been captured by Heracles who brought him from the underworld to be paraded through ancient Greece before he escaped his captivity and returned to his lair.

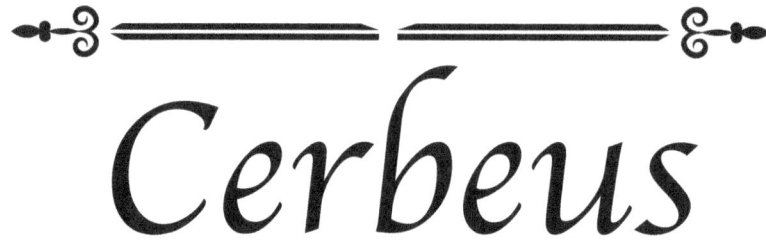

Cerbeus

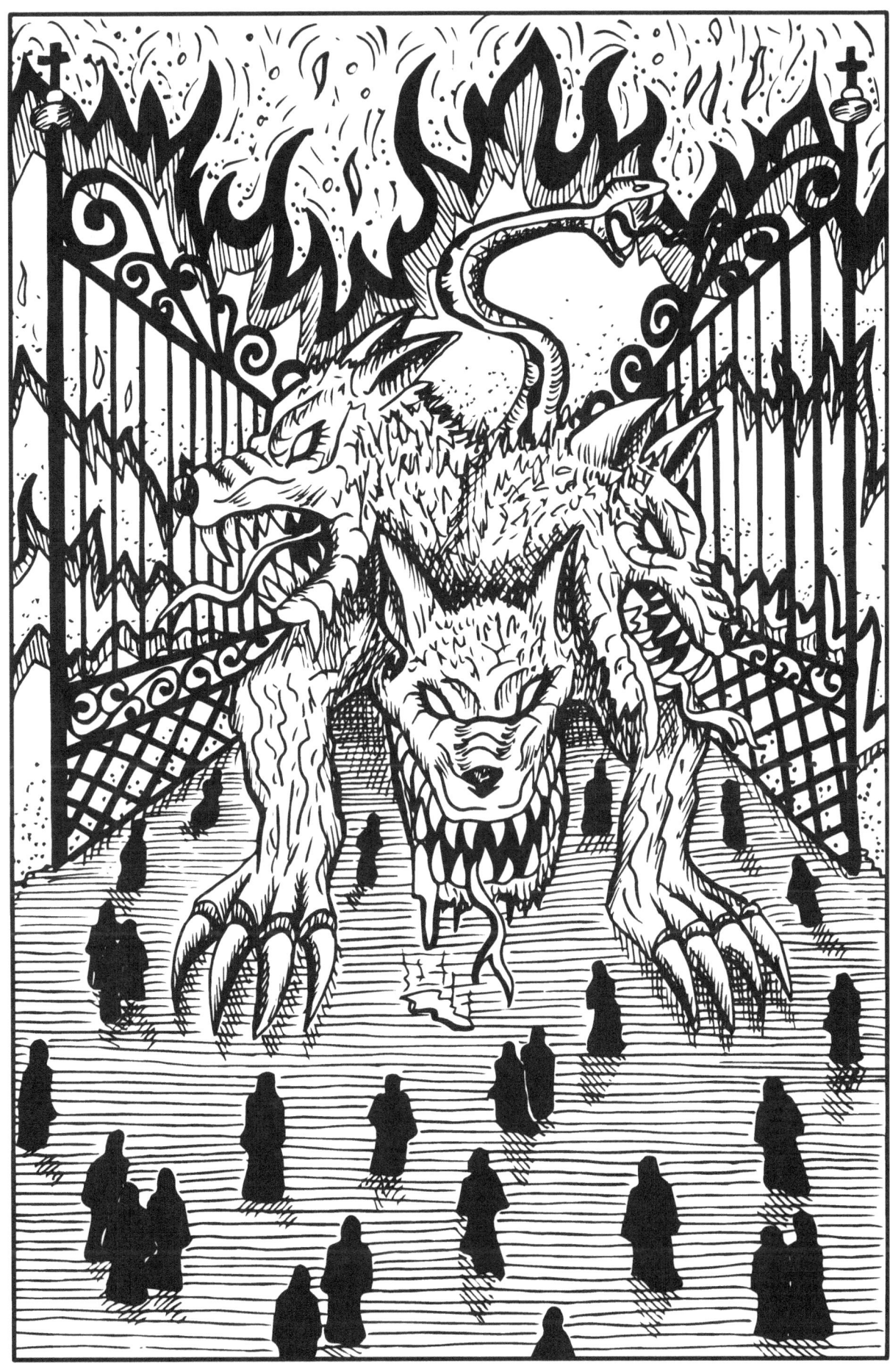

The werewolf is a beast that strikes terror into the heart of all mankind with its ability to shape-shift from a human into a wolf or wolf-like creature.

Werewolves were said to bear tell-tale physical traits even in their human form. These included the meeting of both eyebrows at the bridge of the nose, curved fingernails and low-set ears. A werewolf could also be identified in its human form by cutting the flesh of the accused human to find the fur that would be seen within the wound.

Such was the fear of these legendary beasts, European countries held a series of trials starting in the early 15th century for those accused of werewolfery ,wolf-riding or wolf-charming. The persecution of wolf-charmers continued into the early 18th century.

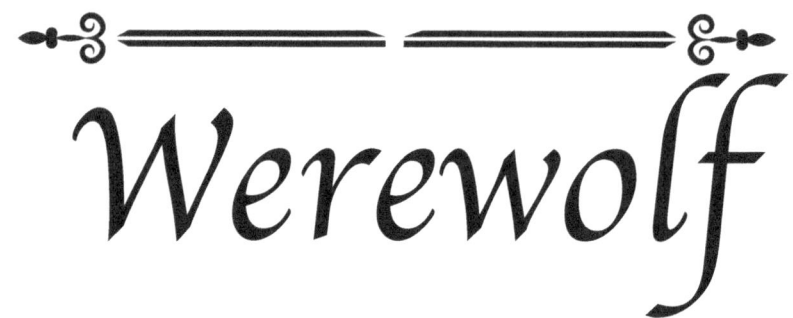

Werewolf

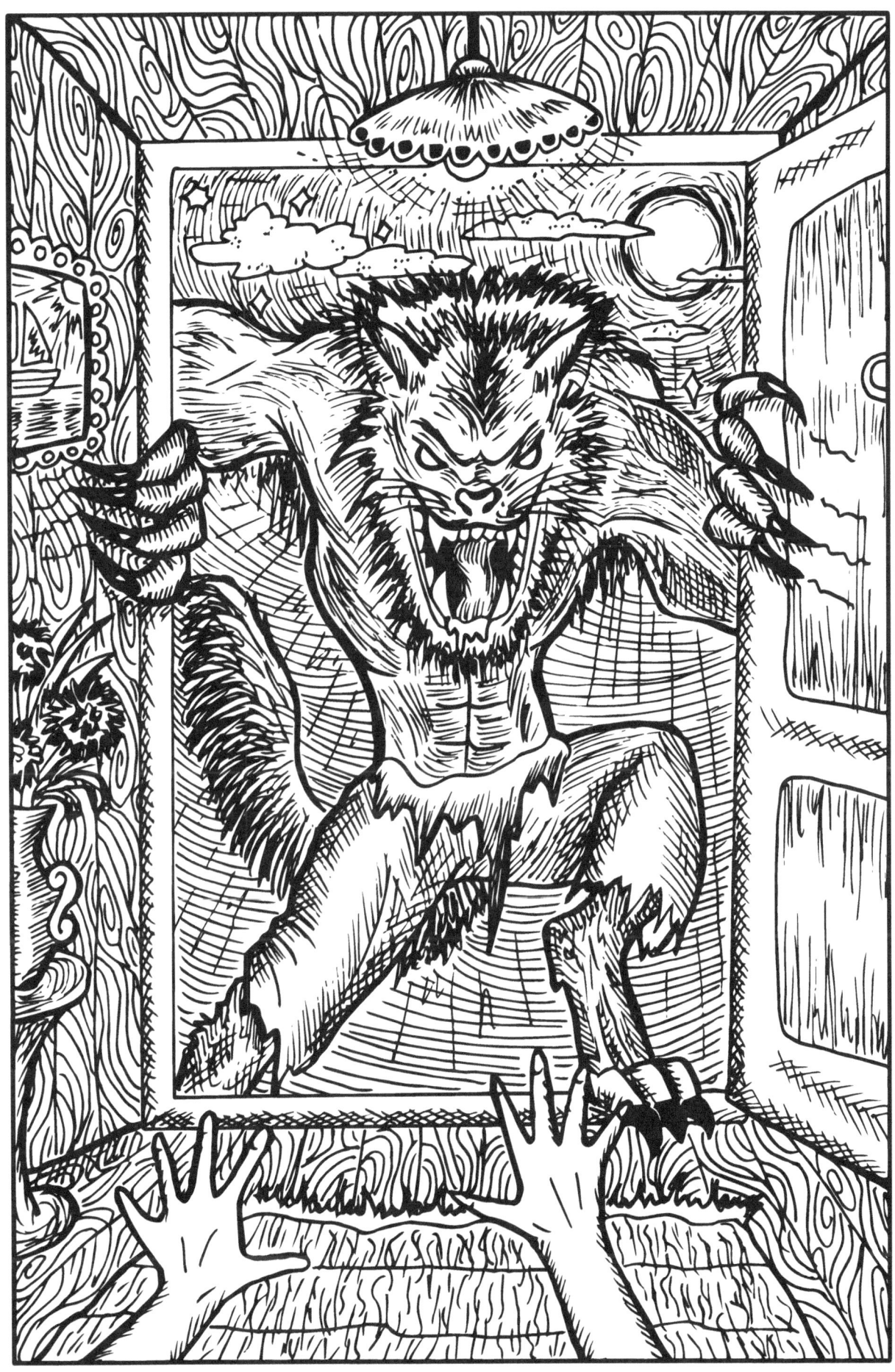

Originating from Persia, Manticore means man-eater. In 1688 writings the Manticore was described as follows:

"the face of a man, the mouth open to the ears with a treble row of teeth beneath and above; long neck, whose greatness, roughness, body and feet are like a Lyon: of a red colour, his tail like the tail of a Scorpion of the Earth, the end armed with a sting, casting forth sharp pointed quills".

Sometimes also portrayed as horned and/or winged its tail could shoot venomous spines to paralyze its victims before devouring them whole – leaving no clothes, bones, or possessions behind.

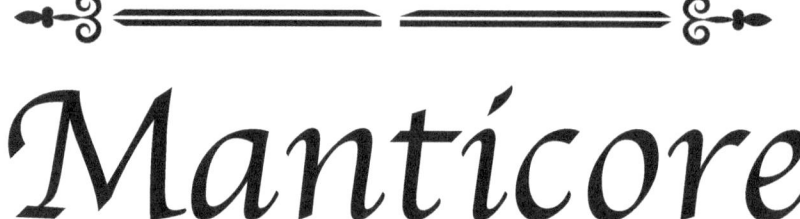

Manticore

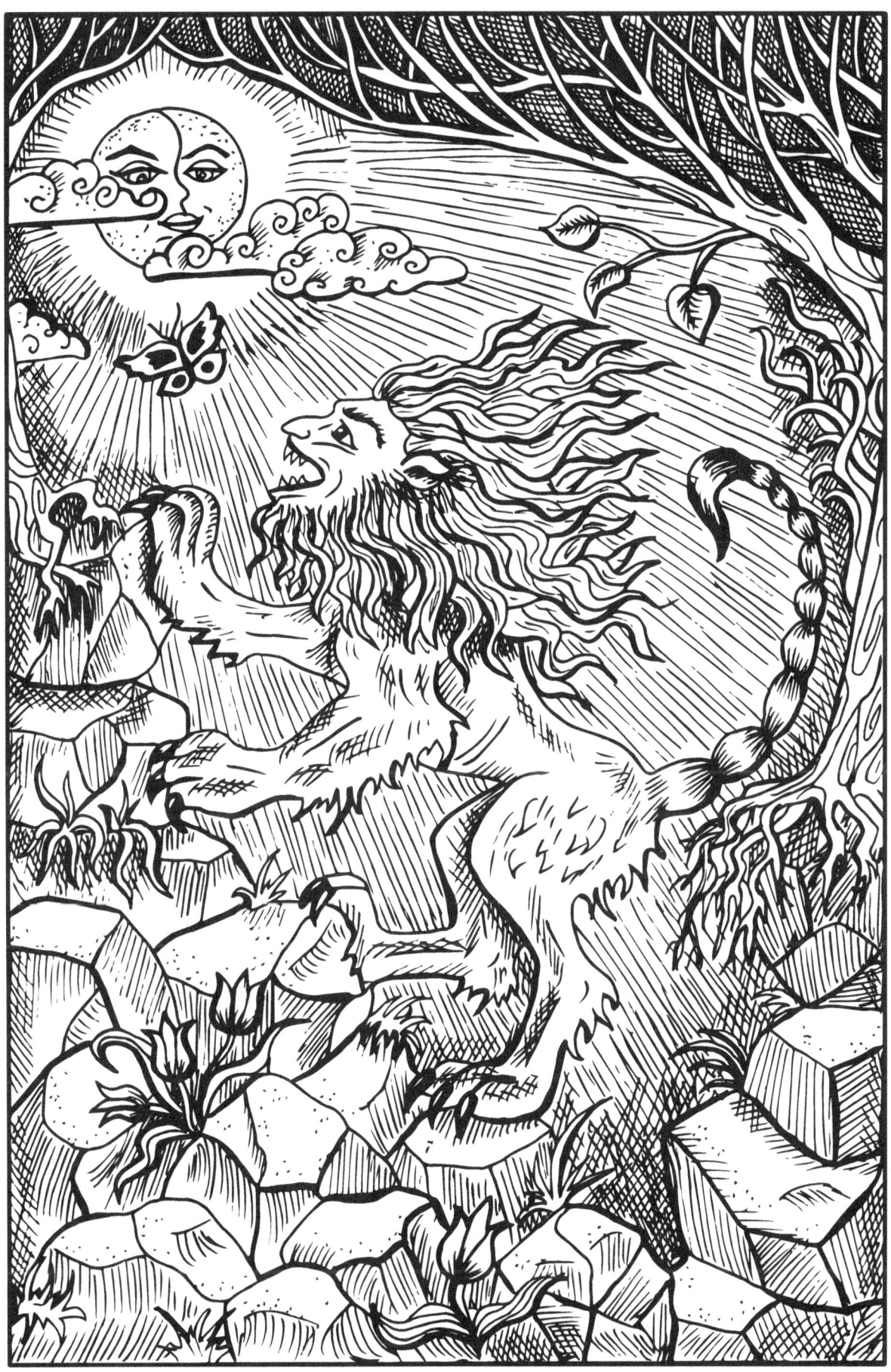

*T*he serpent is one of the oldest of all magnificent mythological symbols. The word is derived from the word Latin 'serpens' - a crawling animal or snake.

Representing both good and evil the legend of the serpent is as old as mankind itself. Connected with vengefulness and vindictiveness, the venom of the serpent is thought to have a fiery quality similar to a fire-spitting dragon. Native Americans were fearful of its reputation and told the story of...

"An evil serpent beast that killed one of their gods' cousins. In revenge the god killed the serpent, but the dying beast, in a last act of vindictiveness, unleashed a great flood which devastated the land".

The Serpent

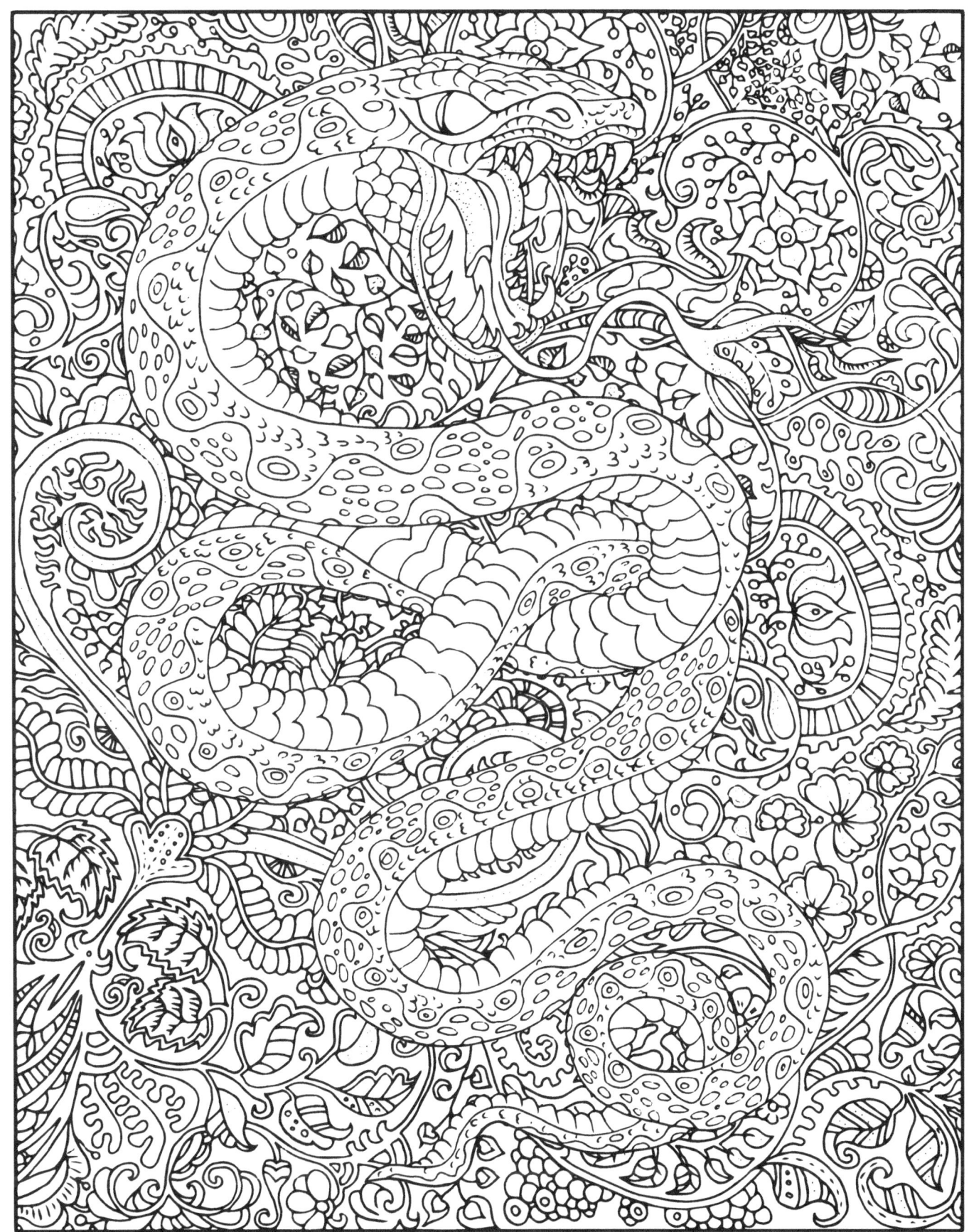

According to Greek mythology the Chimera is fire-breathing beast formed from the parts of more than one animal. It is usually depicted as a lion with a snake-head tail and a sighting of the Chimera was thought to be a sure and ominous omen for disaster.

Appearing in medieval art the Chimera is often depicted as the female embodiment of the deceptive, even satanic forces of raw nature.

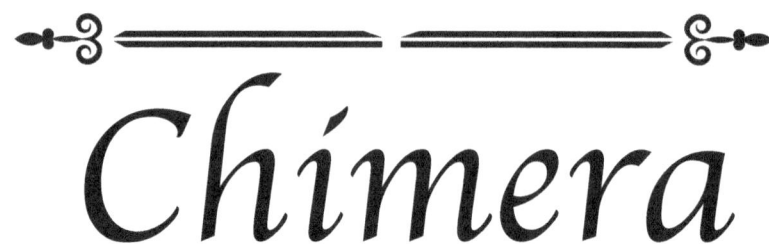

Chimera

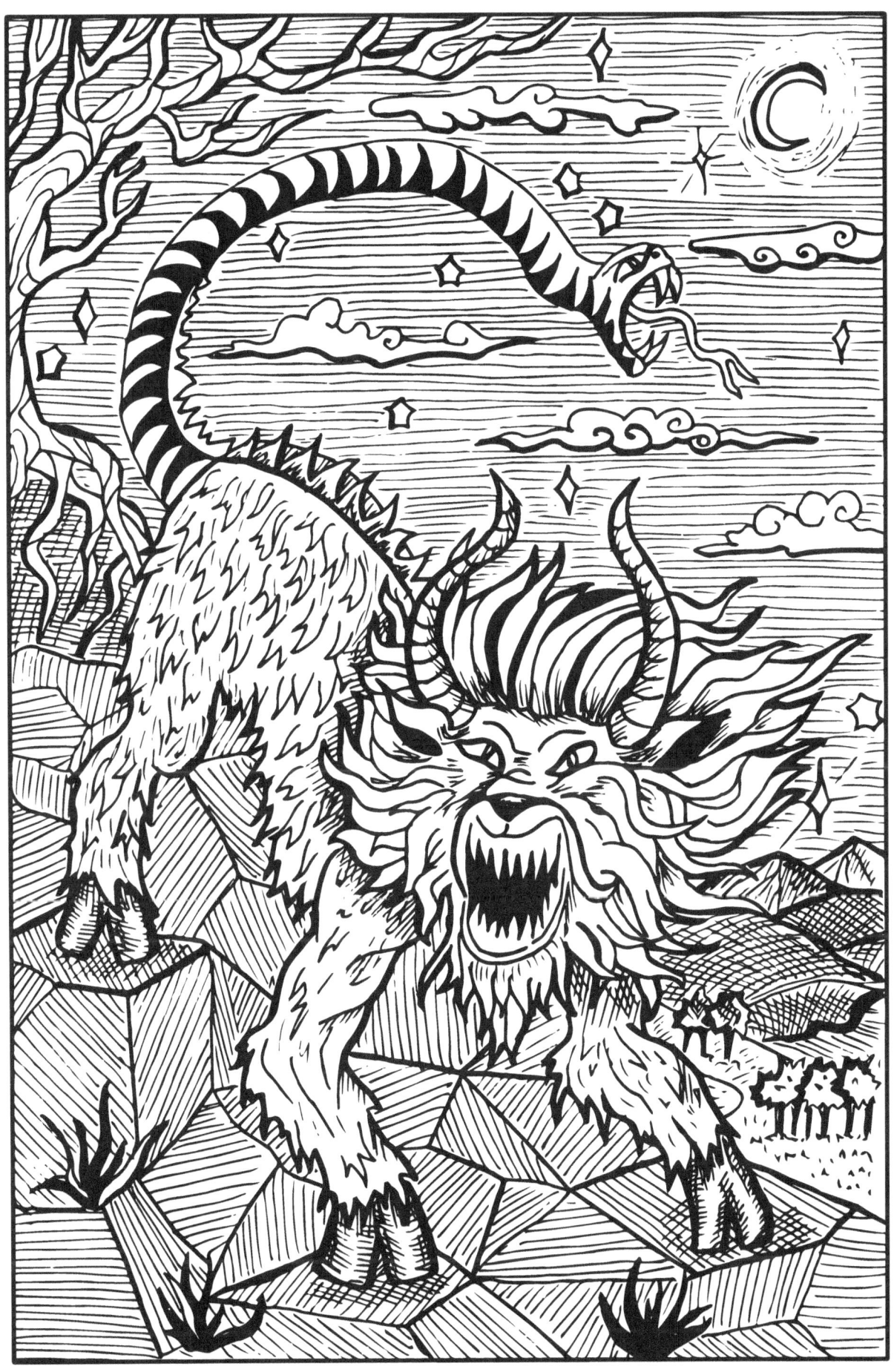

*T*his Egyptian beast is most often associated with mummification and the afterlife. Usually depicted as a canine or a man with a canine head, Anubis was also known as the golden jackal or the African golden wolf.

As one of the gods on the underworld, Anubis was called upon to measure the weighing scale during the "Weighing of the Heart," in which it was decided whether a human soul would be allowed to enter the realm of the dead.

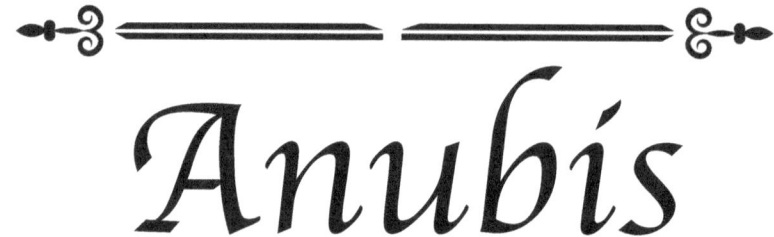

Anubis

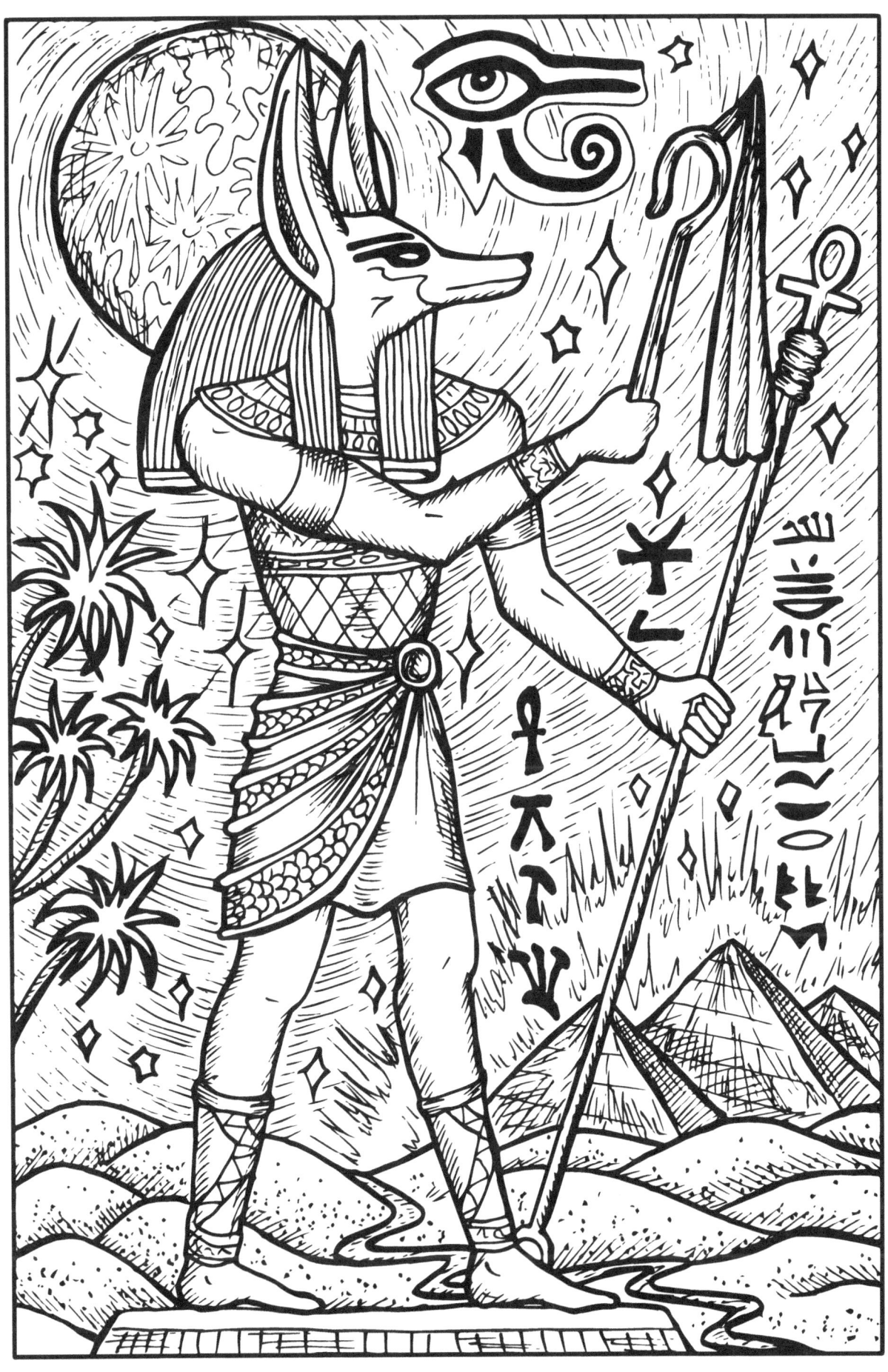

Dragons are legendary fire-spewing beasts with serpentine and reptilian traits which feature in the myths of multiple cultures around the globe.

In both modern and ancient times dragons have preoccupied the human psyche. In medieval times they were used by mapmakers to denote dangerous or unexplored territories often including the phrase "here be dragons" on early maps. In modern times they feature in countless fiction books and movies.

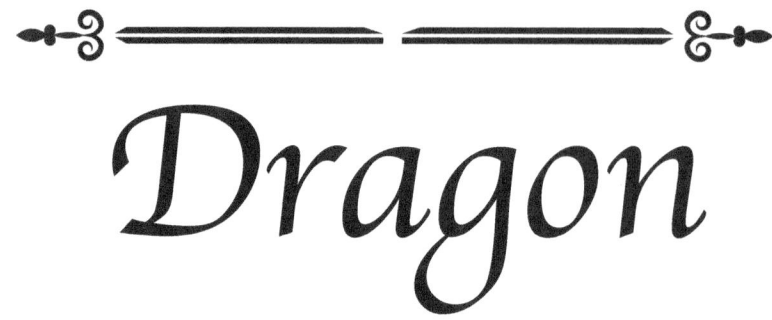

Dragon

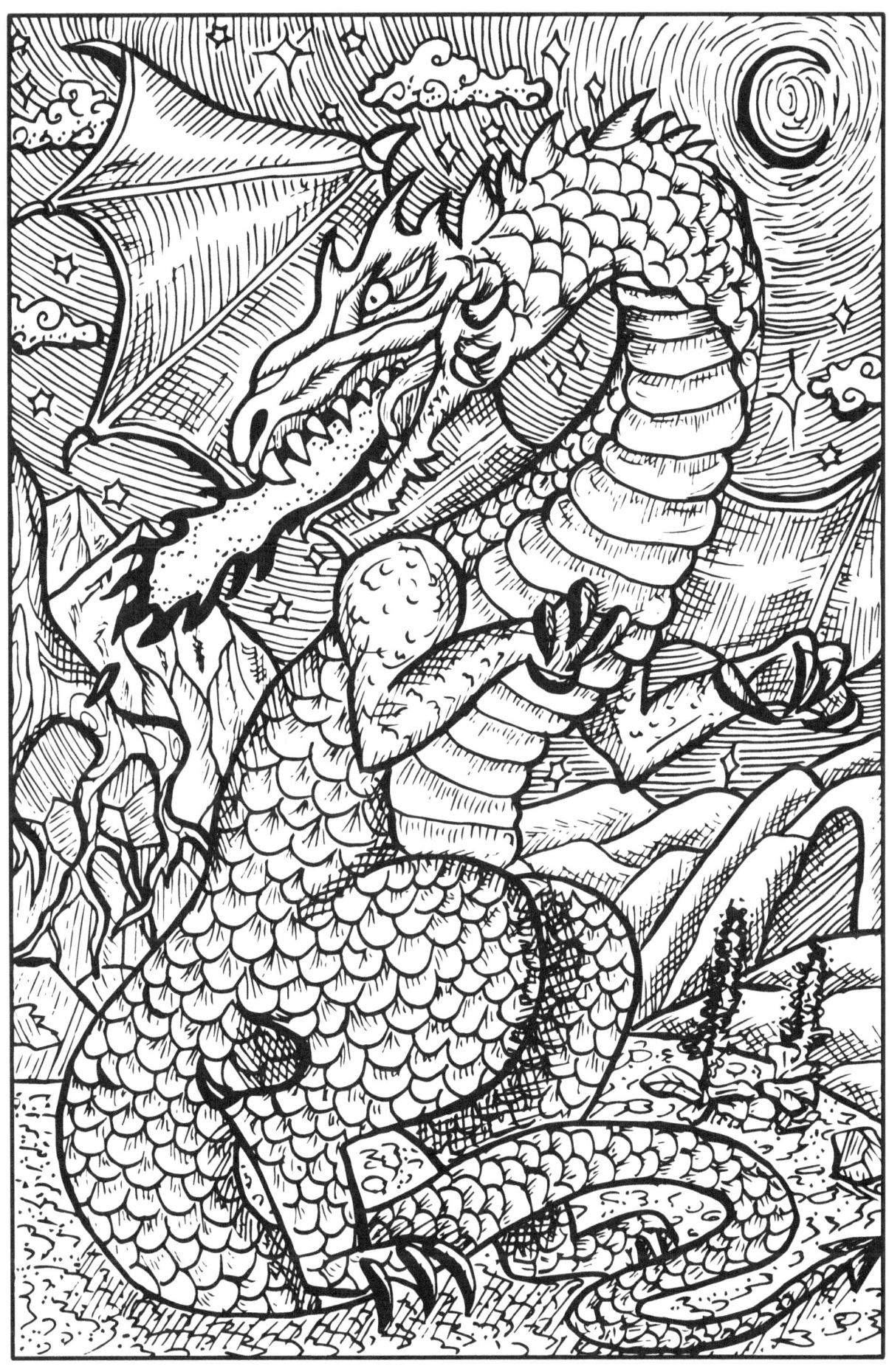

Dragons are amongst the most fearsome and magnificent of all beasts. As such they are often entrusted with guarding some of the most precious of all possessions.

One of the best known is the guarding of the Golden Fleece which, after much effort, Jason successfully retrieved against ferocious dragon resistance.

Dragon Guards

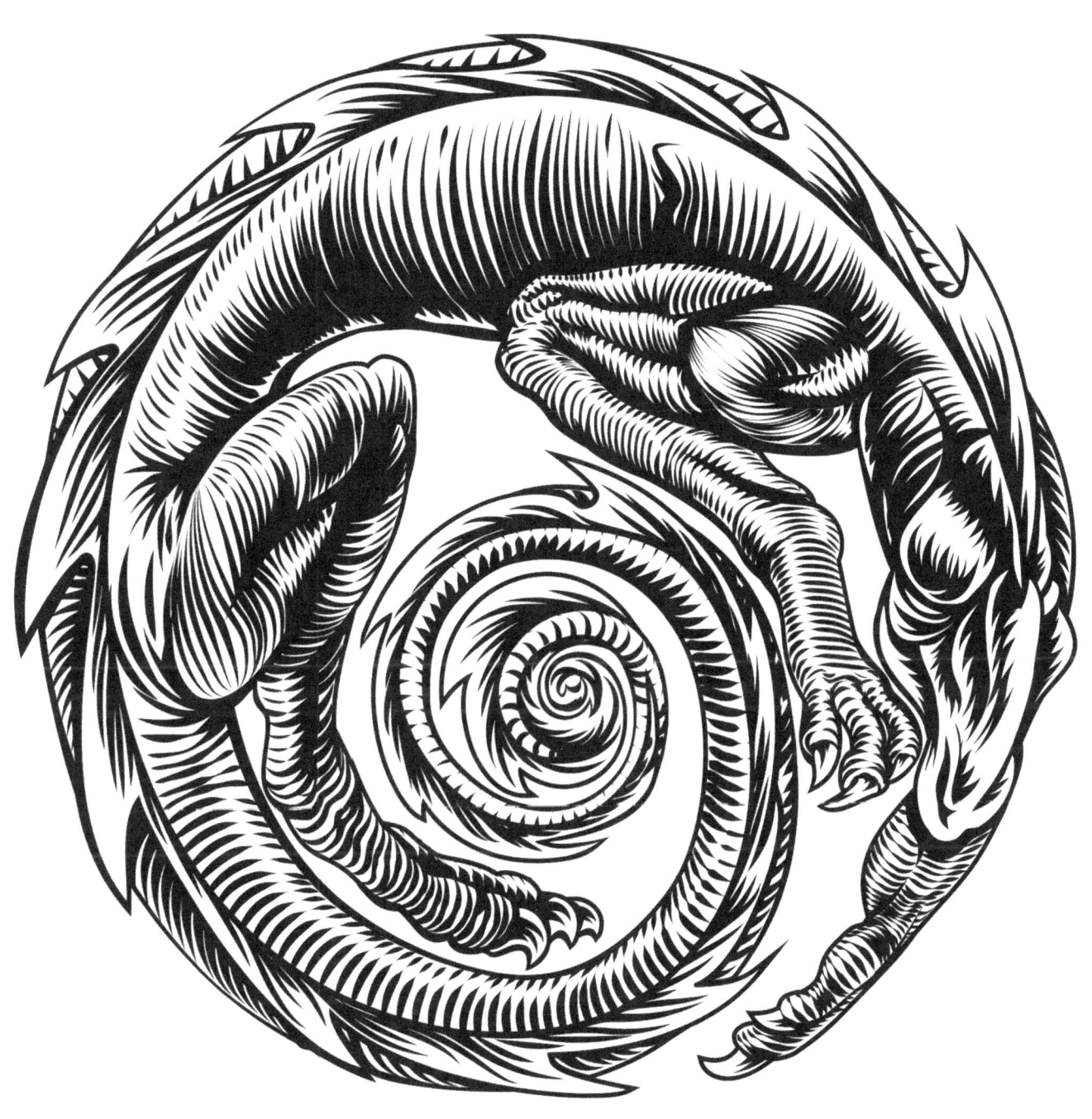

Much of the Orc's mythology stems from the fantasy J. R. R. Tolkien's 'The Lord of the Rings'. Orcs are a brutish, aggressive, repulsive & malevolent species. They are aggressive scavengers with a ferocious taste for cannibalism and human flesh.

Thought to be 'simplistic of mind' they are generally used by those in power rather than holding power themselves. Whilst violent in nature they have a chaotic behavior that can also reveal itself as cowardice.

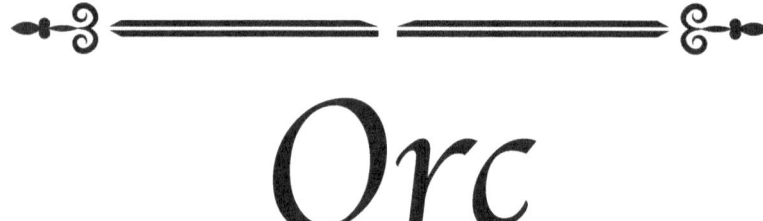

Orc

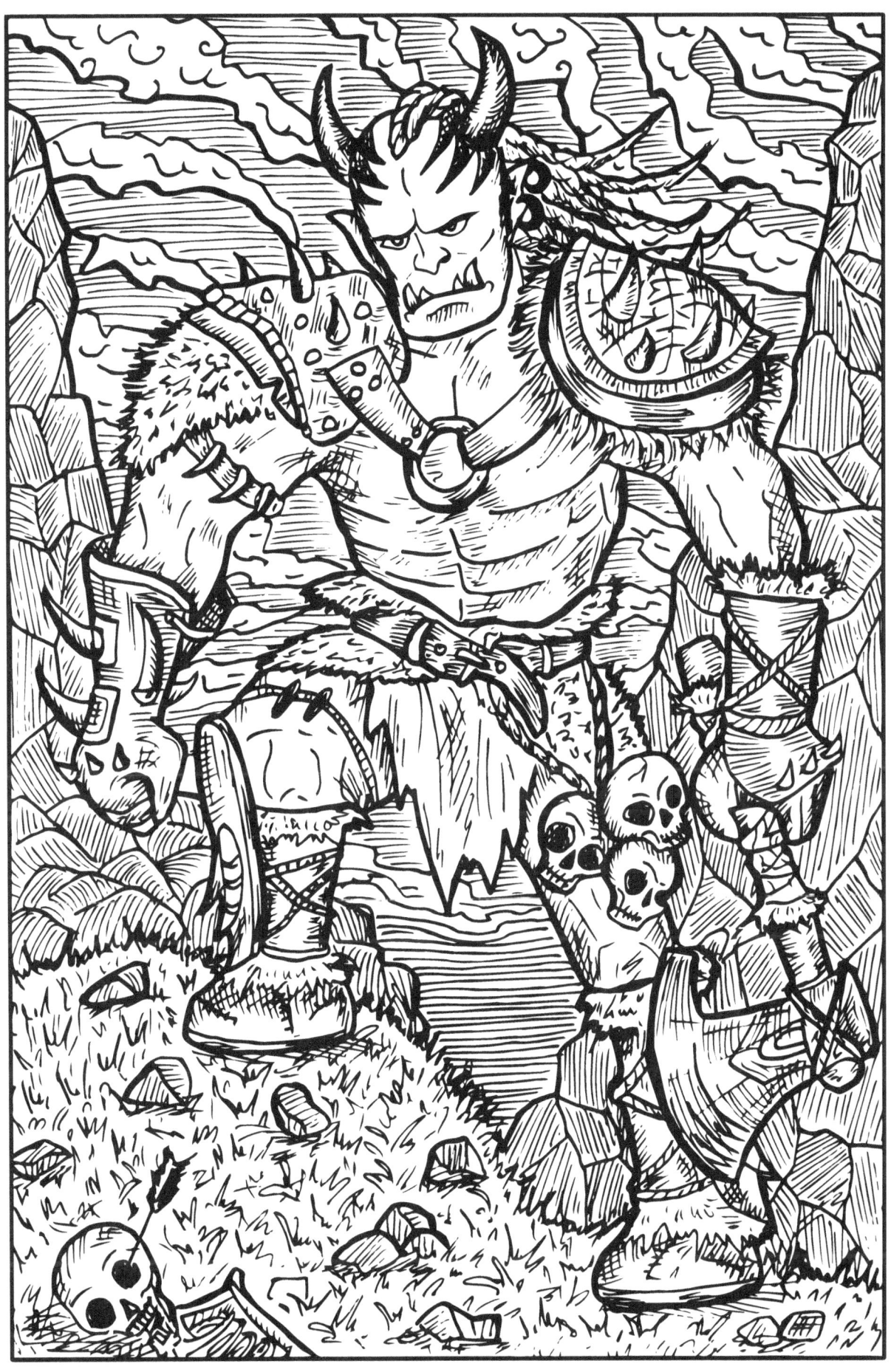

Hailing from Scandinavia The Kraken is a massive legendary sea monster of gigantic proportions. Sometimes likened to a giant octopus or squid the Kraken appears often in fictional works. It was most famously depicted in Alfred Tennyson's 1830 sonnet:

Below the thunders of the upper deep;
Far far beneath in the abysmal sea,
His ancient, dreamless, uninvaded sleep
The Kraken sleepeth: faintest sunlights flee
About his shadowy sides; above him swell
Huge sponges of millennial growth and height;
And far away into the sickly light

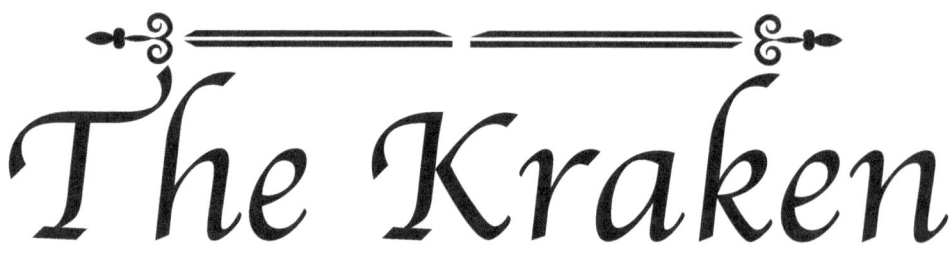

The Kraken

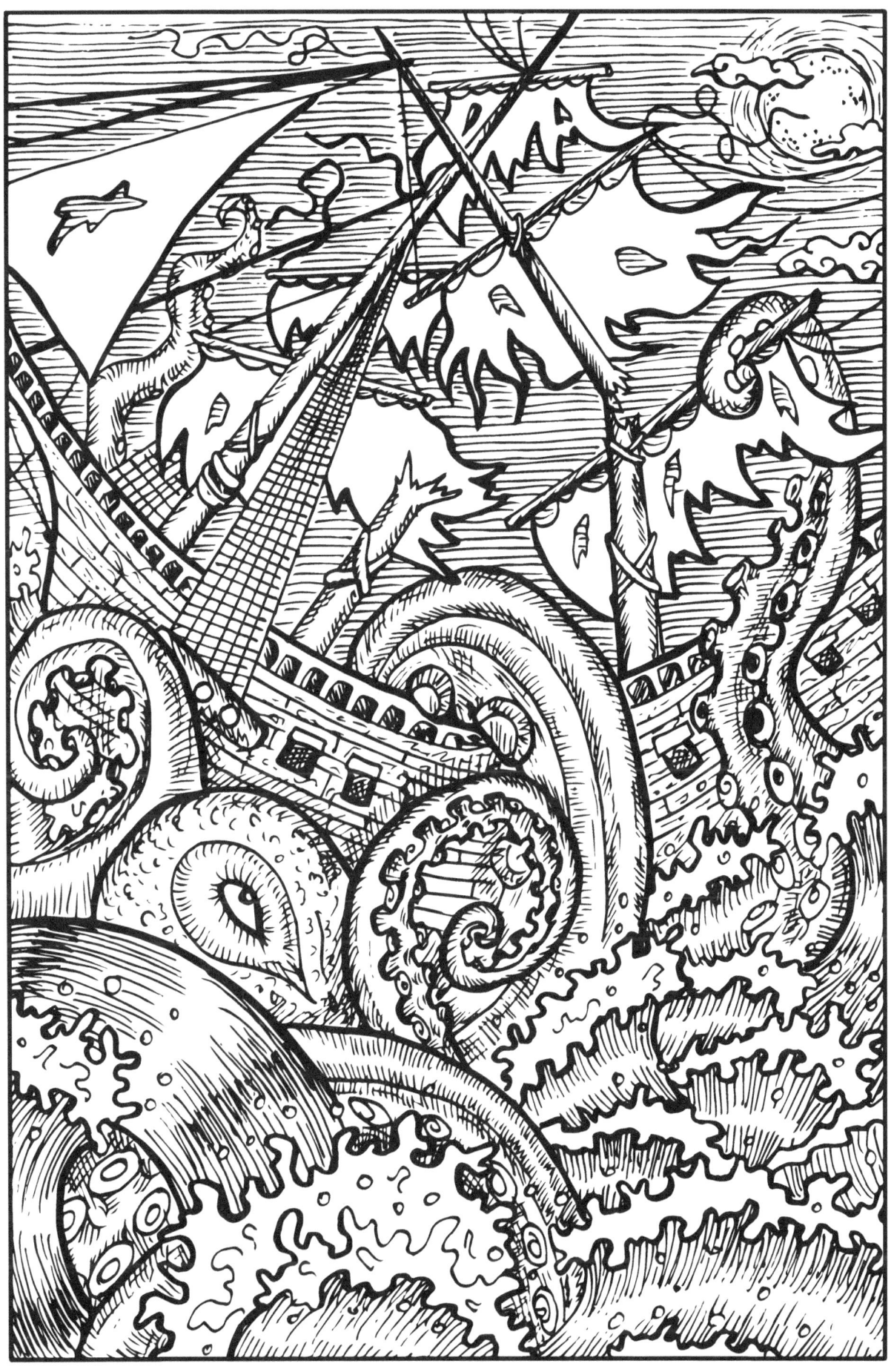

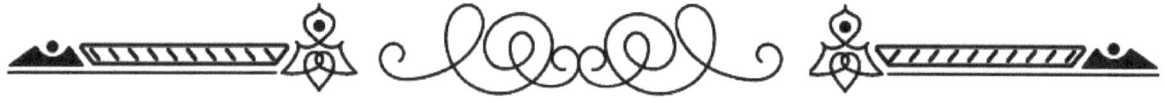

*P*art man and part bull the mighty Minotaur is a beast of ancient Greek mythology. Conceived from the union between a woman and a bull, when the Minotaur was born, he would only eat humans.

The Minotaur dwelt at the center of the Labyrinth, which had been built on the command of King Minos of Crete. Human sacrifices where sent to him there until he was eventually killed by Theseus who found his way in and out of the deadly labyrinth marking the trail with a ball of thread.

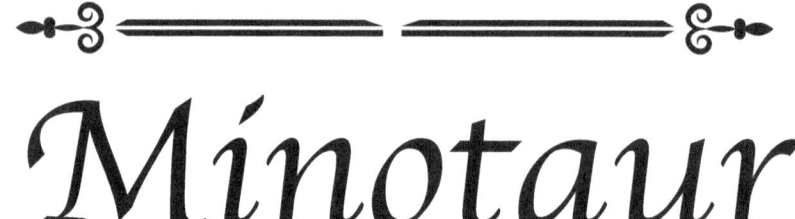

Minotaur

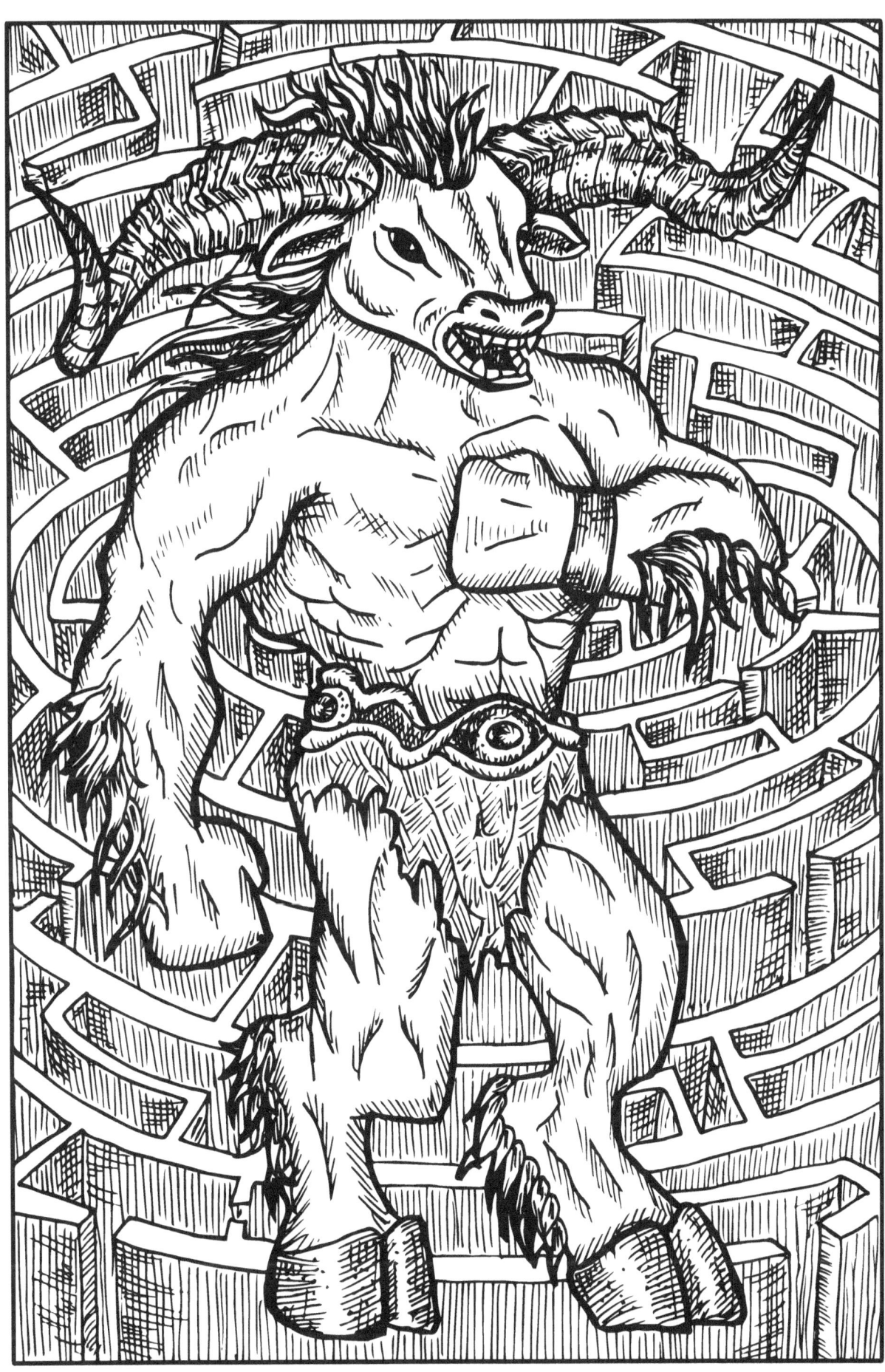

*T*ranslated as "feathered serpent" the Quetzalcoatl was worshiped as an Aztec deity. During the period (900–1519 AD), the worship of the feathered serpent was centered around the Mexican religious 'mecca' of Cholula. It is in this period that the deity is known to have been named "Quetzalcoatl" by his Nahua followers.

In the 1982 the Quetzalcoatl reached modern day movie-star status as the main character of the film 'Q' as the beast who terrorizes New York City.

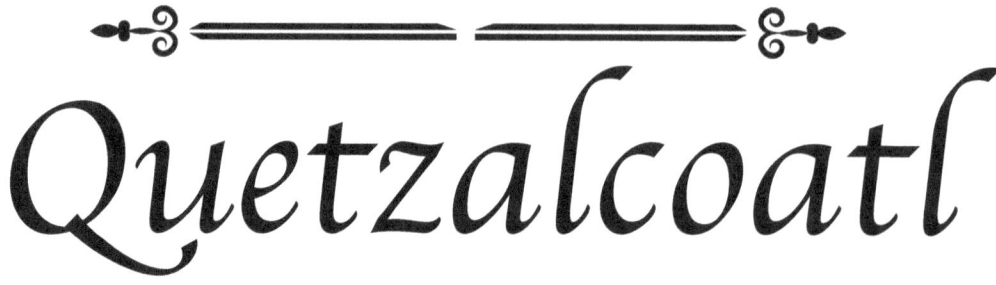

Quetzalcoatl

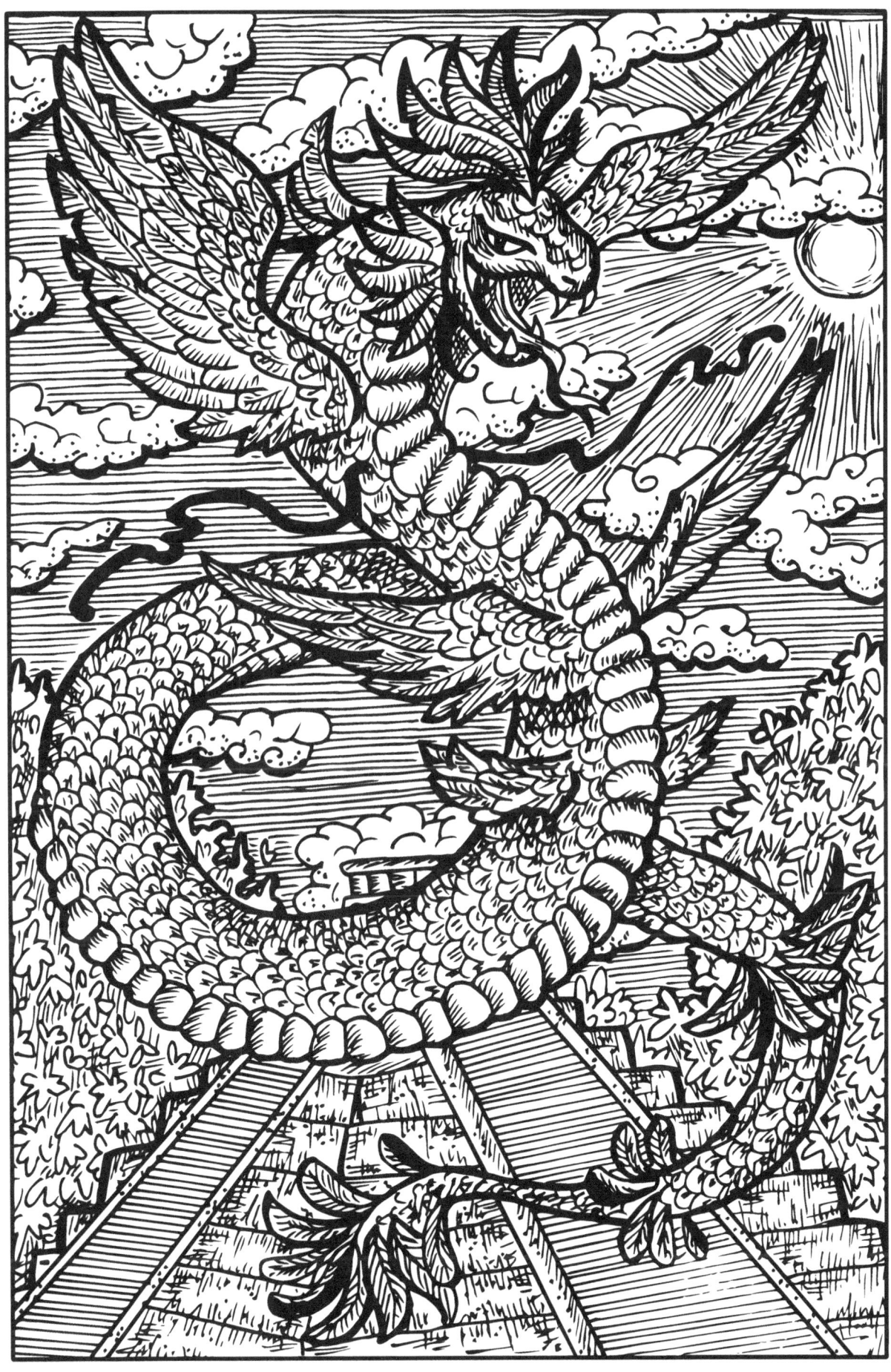

Another of the Greek mythological beasts Hydra was a giant water snake with many heads that lived in a swamp near Lerna in the land of Argos.

Reports of the number of heads of this feared beast fluctuates between five and one hundred, although it is most often depicted as a nine or ten headed monster. Hydra was though to be immortal as it was impossible to kill all of the animal's heads.

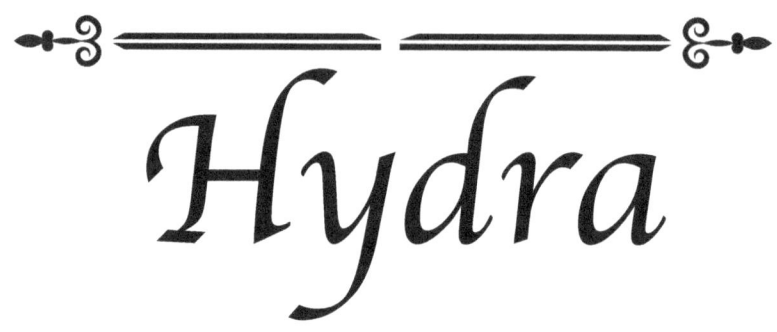

Hydra

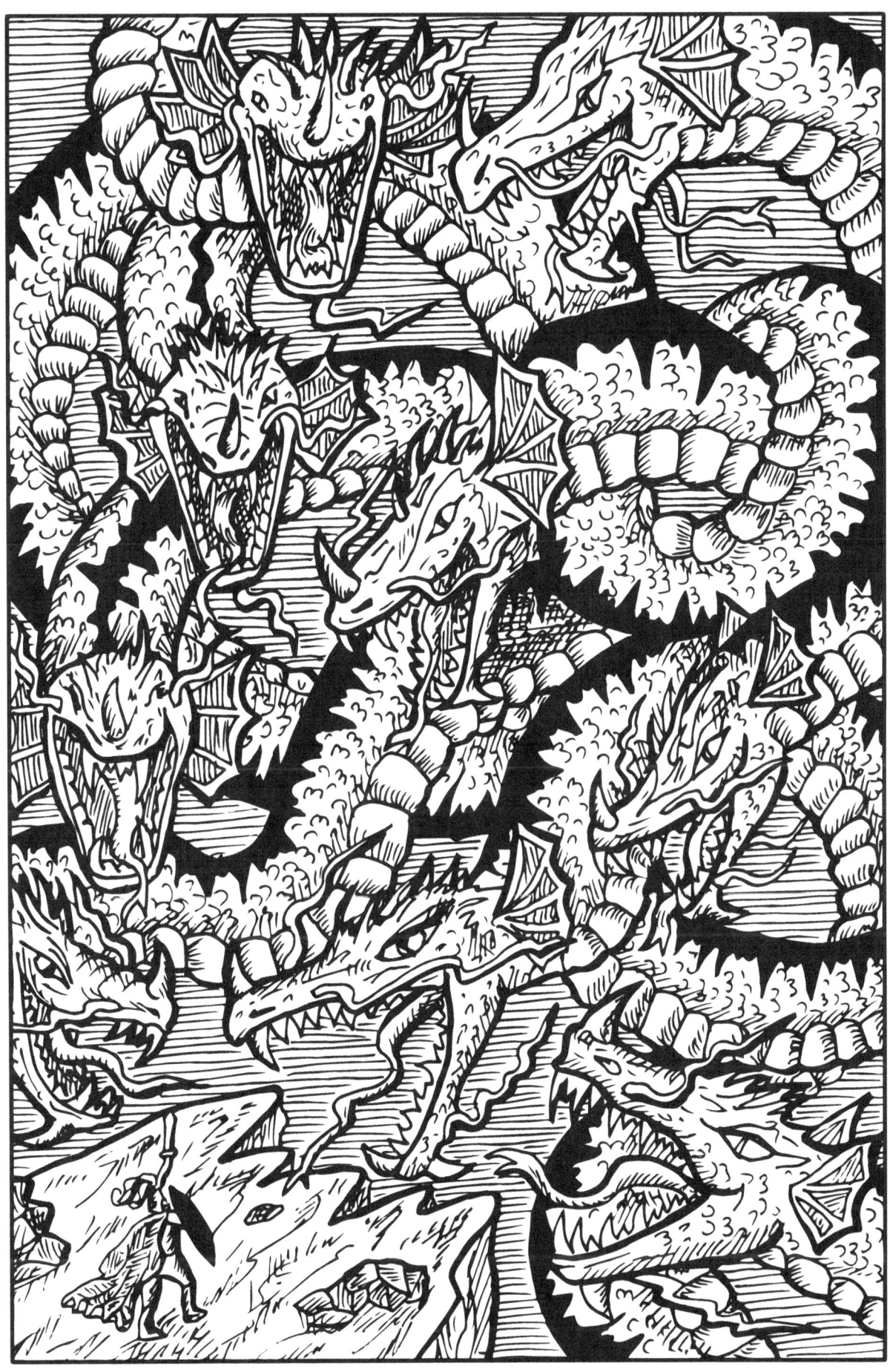

Most often found in cemeteries, Ghouls are monsters or evil spirits who rob graves to feed on dead bodies. Thought to have originally derived from Muslim legend, ghouls are also cannibalistic as well as being fans of human flesh.

Other cultures believe ghouls are capable of shape-shifting , able to imitate the form of other beings. Middle Eastern mythology calls ghouls the evil female spirit of the desert.

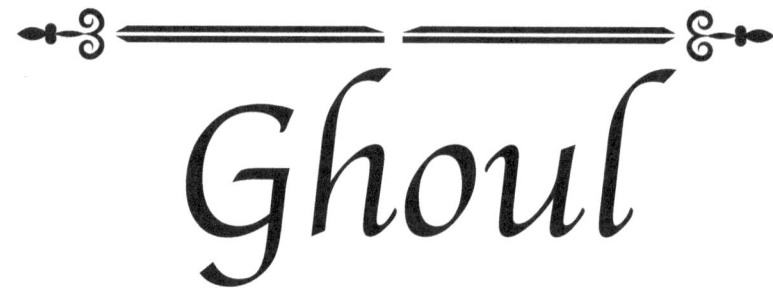

Ghoul

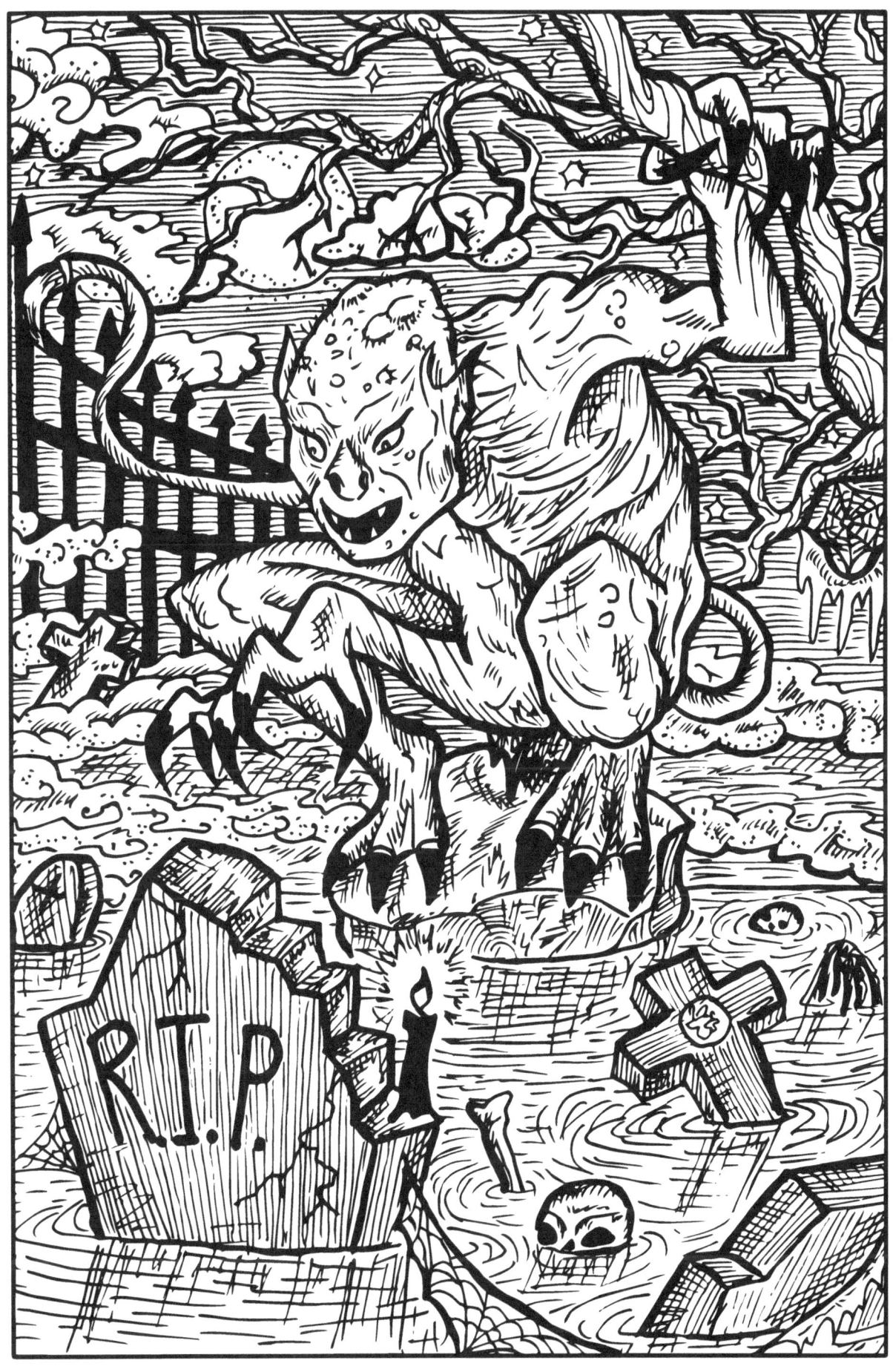

Wild and uncontrollable, imps originate from Germanic folklore.
Likened to a small goblin they are often portrayed as mischievous rather than evil and in some regions they were known as the assistants of of the gods, fond of playing tricks and mis-leading people.

Most of the time imps would cause people nothing more than frustrations with their tricks, but not everything was harmless fun as they would also sometimes switch babies or lead travellers into dangerous territories. Imps were often thought of as being immortal, although certain weapons and enchantments could harm them.

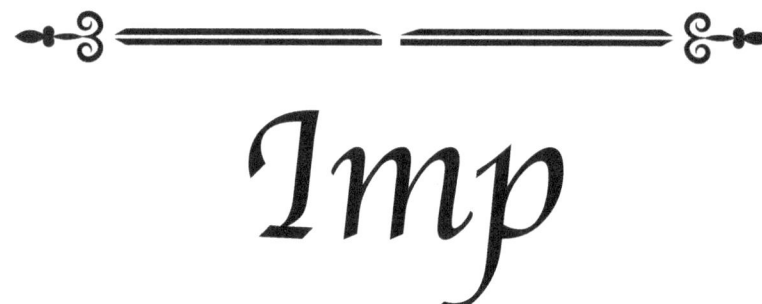

Imp

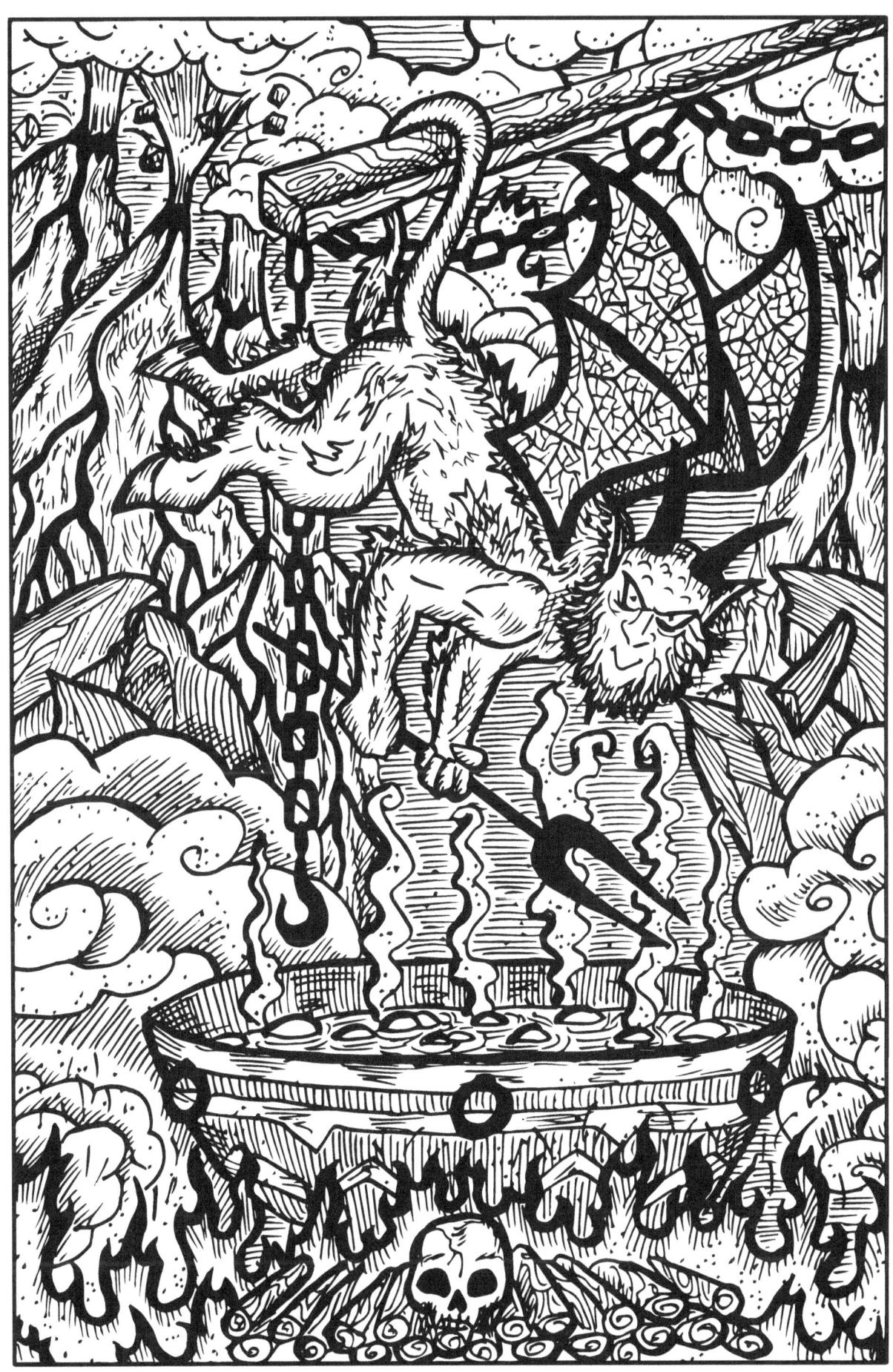

Cetus in ancient Greek is a large fish, whale or sea monster. In Greek mythology Perseus rescued Andromeda who under the wrath of Poseidon, god of the sea, was to be devoured by Cetus. It is said Perseus slayed Cetus with his sword into its back while in another he used the head of Medusa to turn Cetus into stone.

Cetus is also a star constellation also often called 'the whale'.

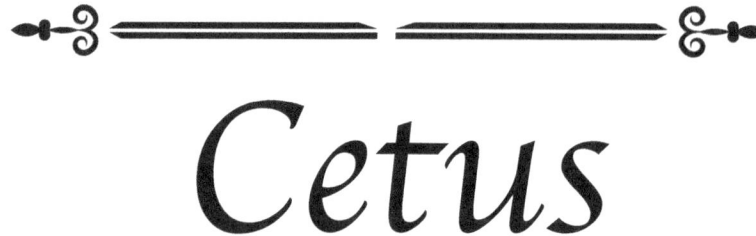

Cetus

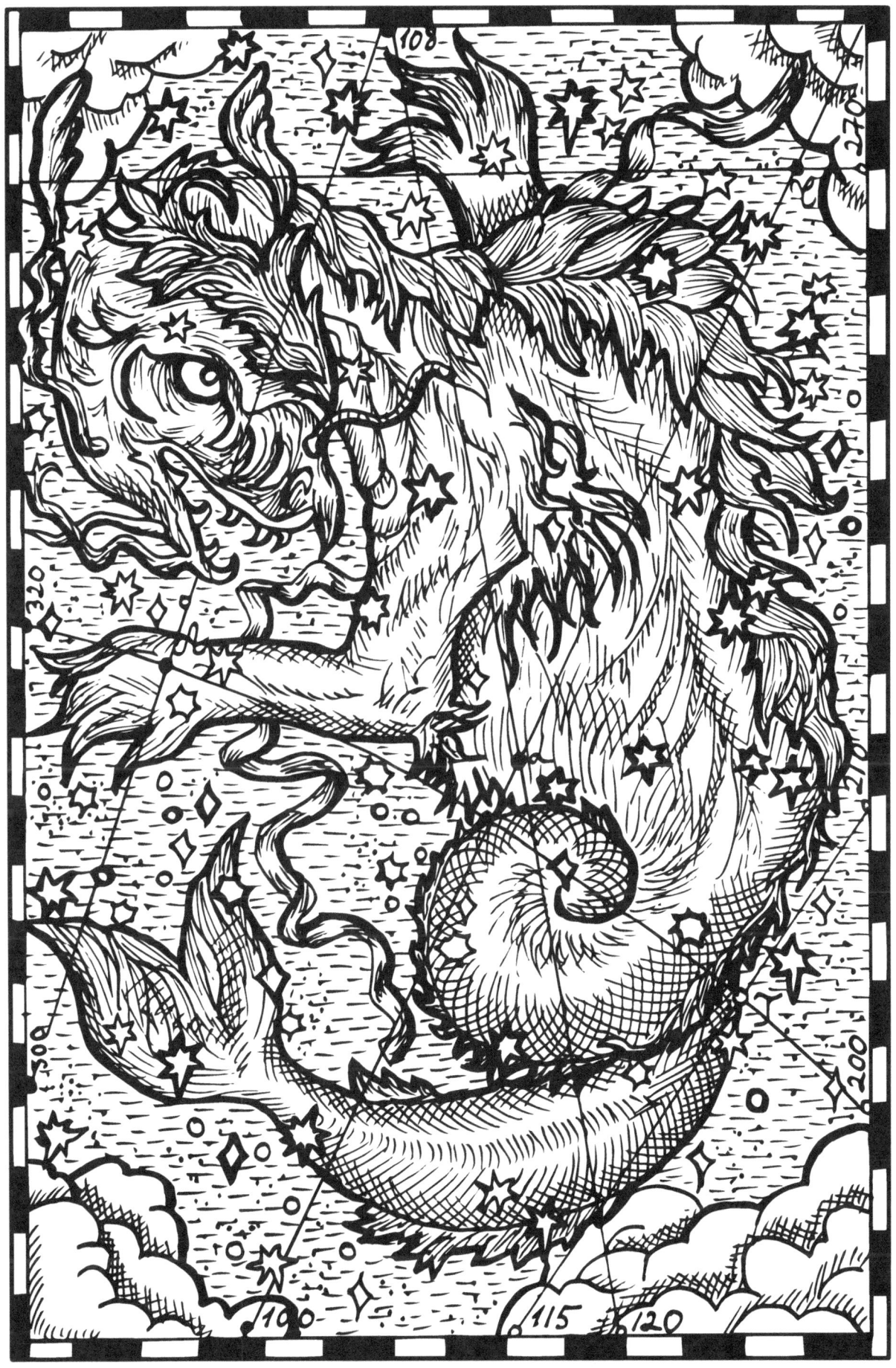

The legend of the Loch Ness Monster still preoccupies the modern psyche, with countless people still making daily trips out on the Loch's dark deep waters to try to catch of glimpse of this magnificent beast.

Known locally (and affectionately) as Nessie the monster is an aquatic being which dwells in the largest loch of the Scottish Highlands. Thought of as a gentle soul this beloved beast has a long neck with one or more humps protruding from the water when it swims. There are no reports of it ever attacking humans or capsizing boats.

Loch Ness Monster

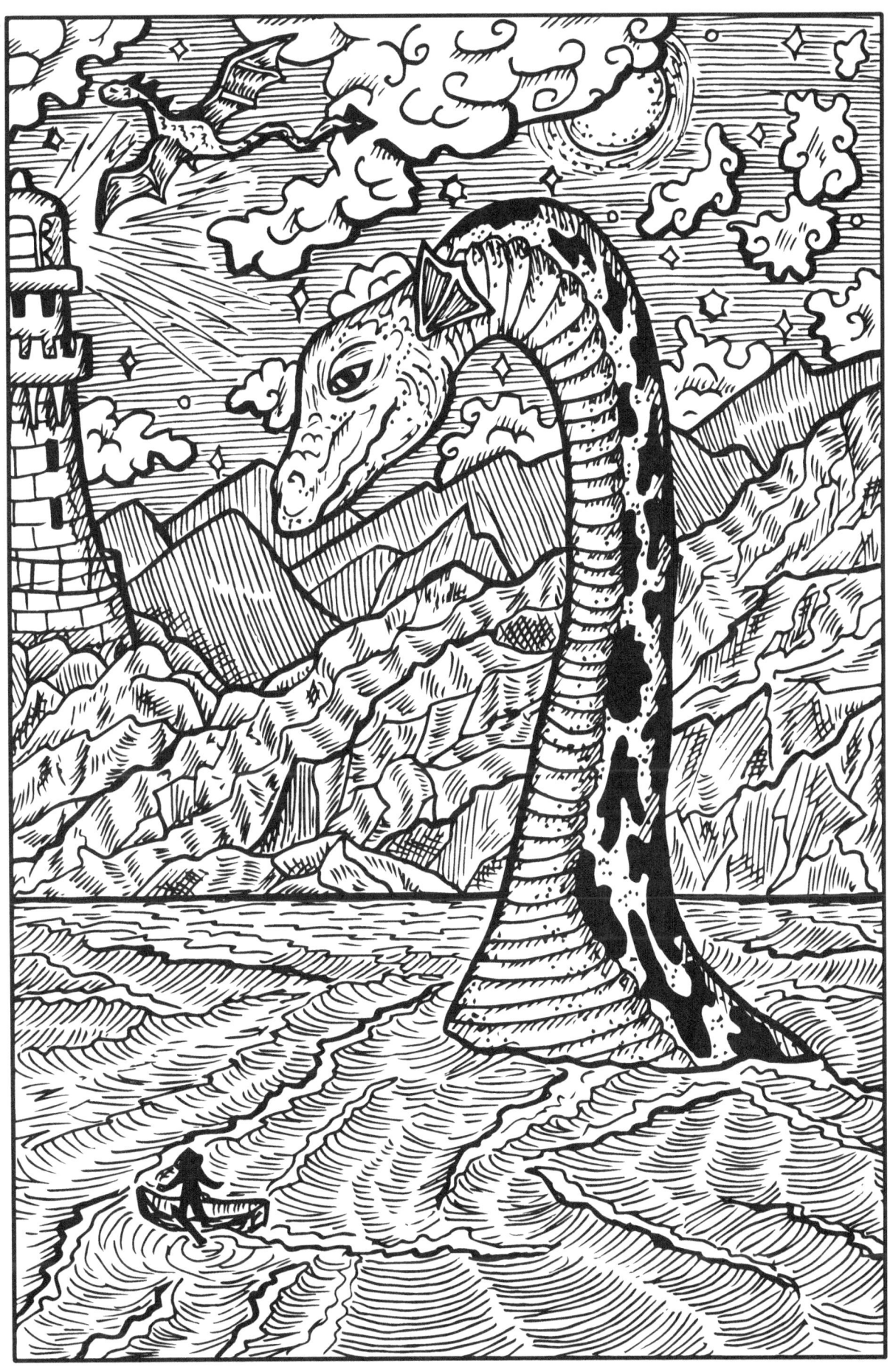

*T*he dark origins of Lilith lie in Babylonian demonology, where amulets and incantations were used to counter the sinister powers of this winged spirit who preyed on pregnant women and infants.

It is believed she wandered the earth for 4,000 years figuring in the mythic imaginations of writers, artists and poets. In the bible she makes a single appearance as a wilderness demon shunned by the prophet Isaiah...

"She shall become an abode for jackals and a haunt for ostriches. Wildcats shall meet with desert beasts, satyrs shall call to one another; There shall the Lilith repose, and find for herself a place to rest."

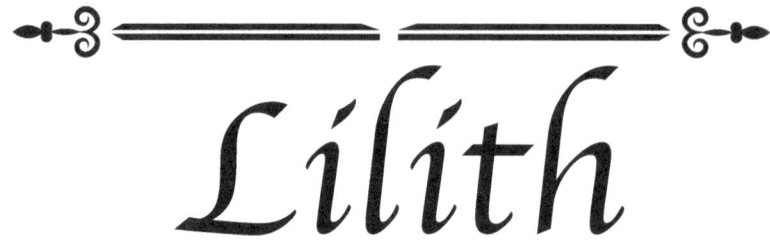

Lilith

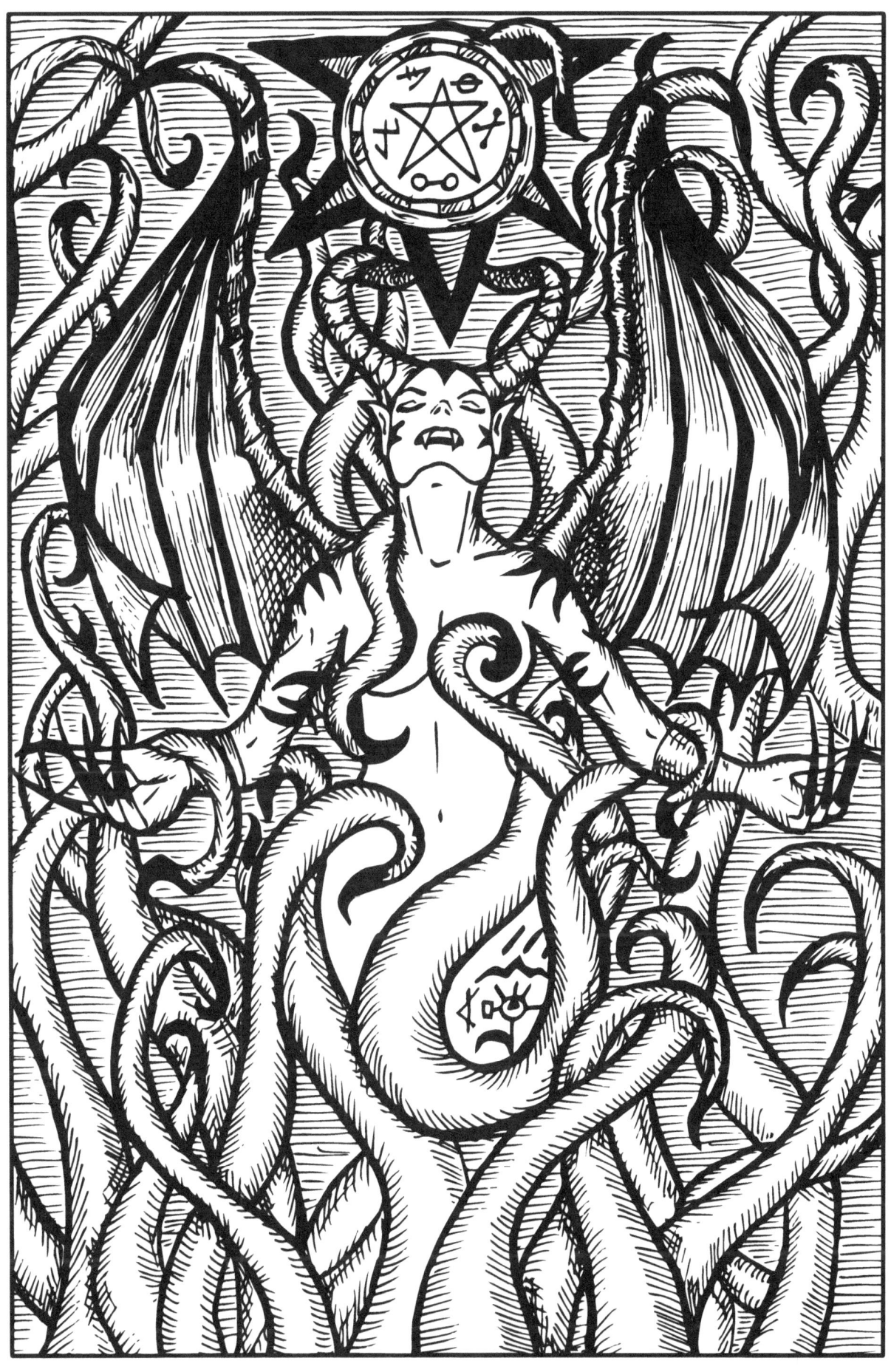

Arachne was a talented weaver who challenged the ancient Greek goddess Athena to a weaving competition. Zeus, as the judge of the contest, decreed whoever lost would not be allowed to touch a spindle or the loom again – which would have been a great punishment for either party.

Athena won and Arachne was devastated. Out of pity, Athena transformed her into a spider, so she could continue weaving without having to break her oath.

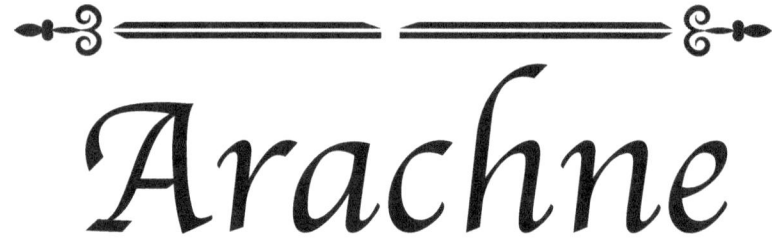

Arachne

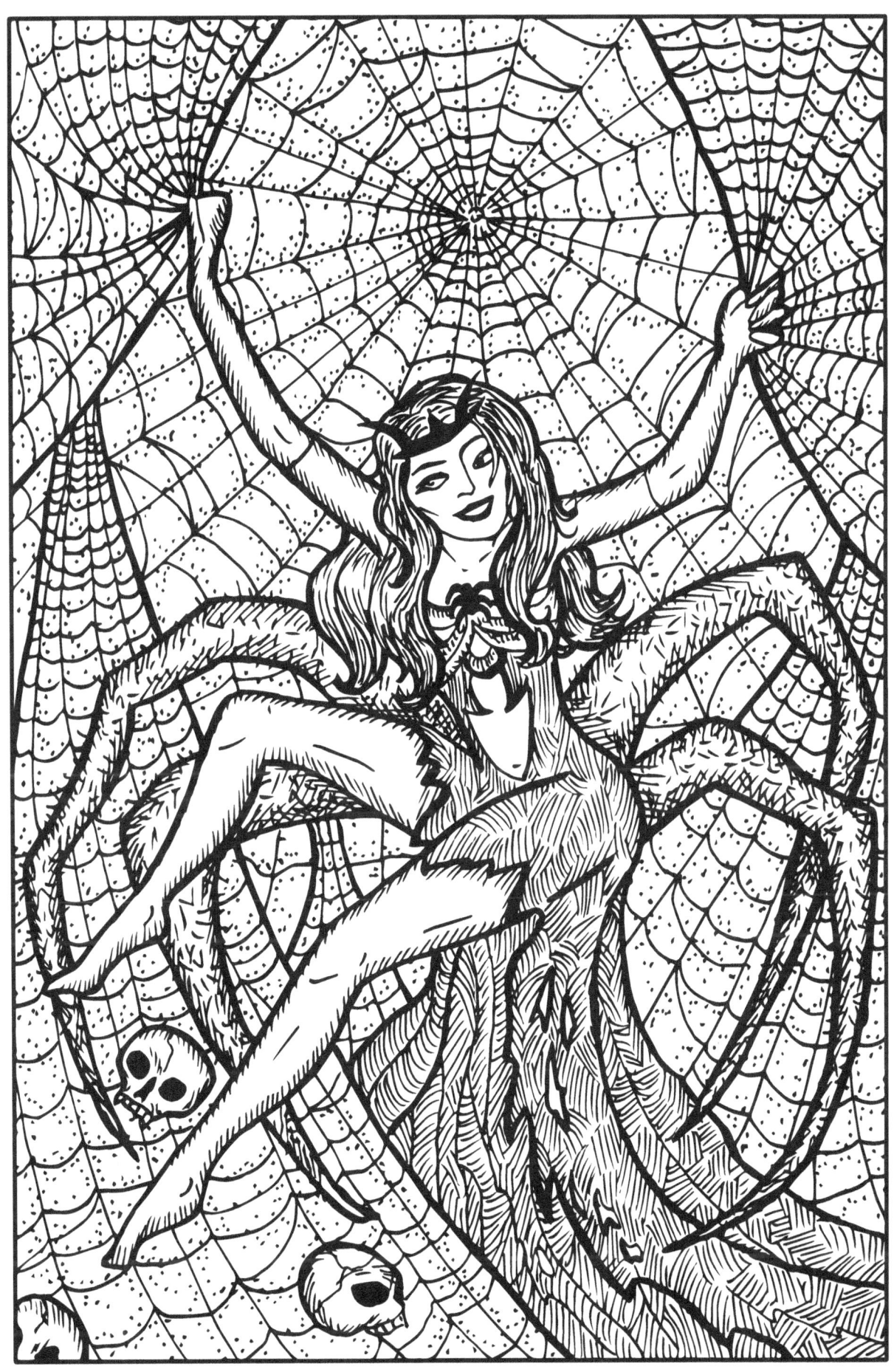

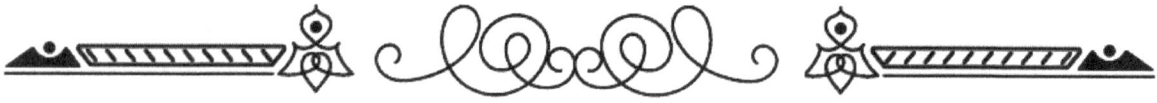

The Ouroboros is a Greek word meaning 'tail devourer,' and is one of the oldest symbols in the world. The Serpent biting its own tail is first seen as early as 1600 years BC in Egypt as a symbol of the sun, and represented the travels of the sun disk. The Greeks gave it its name, Ouroboros, which means devouring its tail.

The Ouroboros appears in many other cultures - the Serpent Jormungand of Norse legend grew so large that it could encircle the world and grasp its tail in its teeth. It guarded the Tree of Life, and is often depicted as an ouroboros.

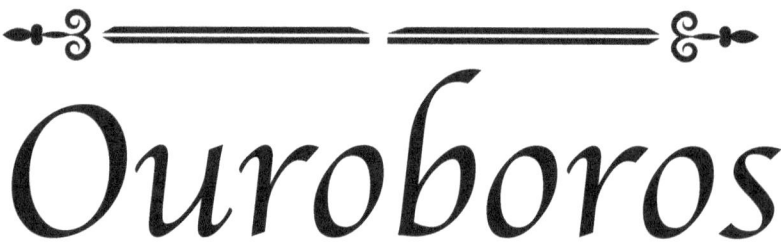

Ouroboros

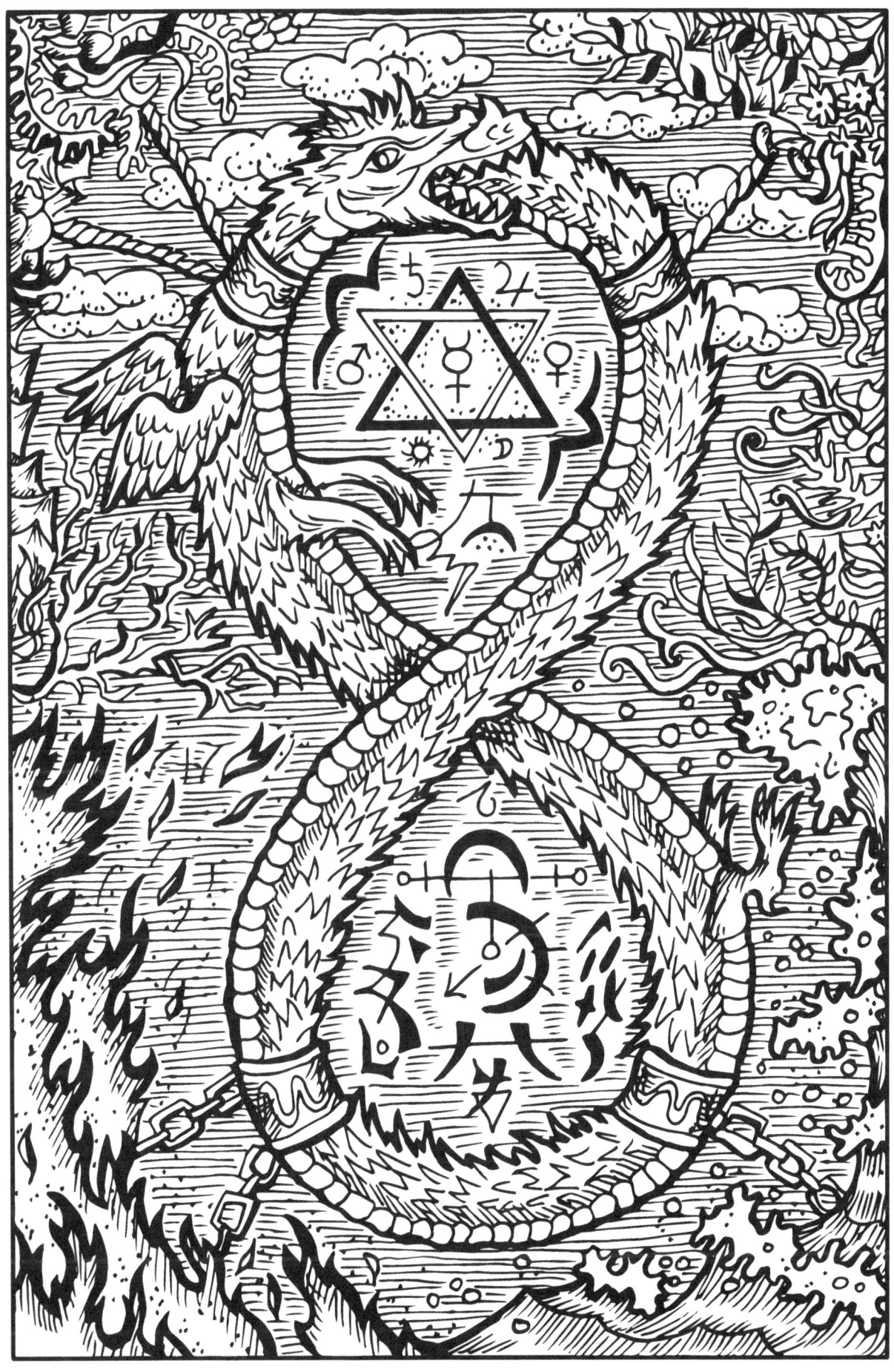

Half-woman and half-snake this beautiful ancient Greek beast is thought to have lived alone in a cave.
She was described as a fierce goddess. A flesh-eating monster who was also 'irresistible'. Her appearance was a paradox 'half a nymph with glancing eyes and fair cheeks, and half again a huge snake, great and awful, with speckled skin'.

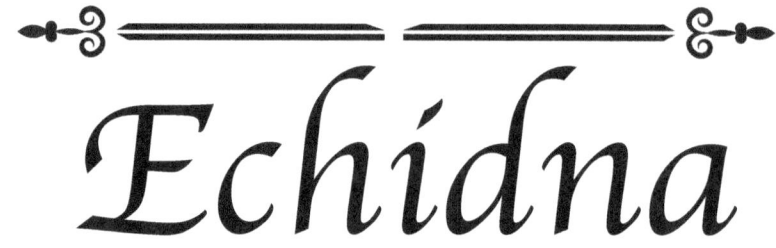

Echidna

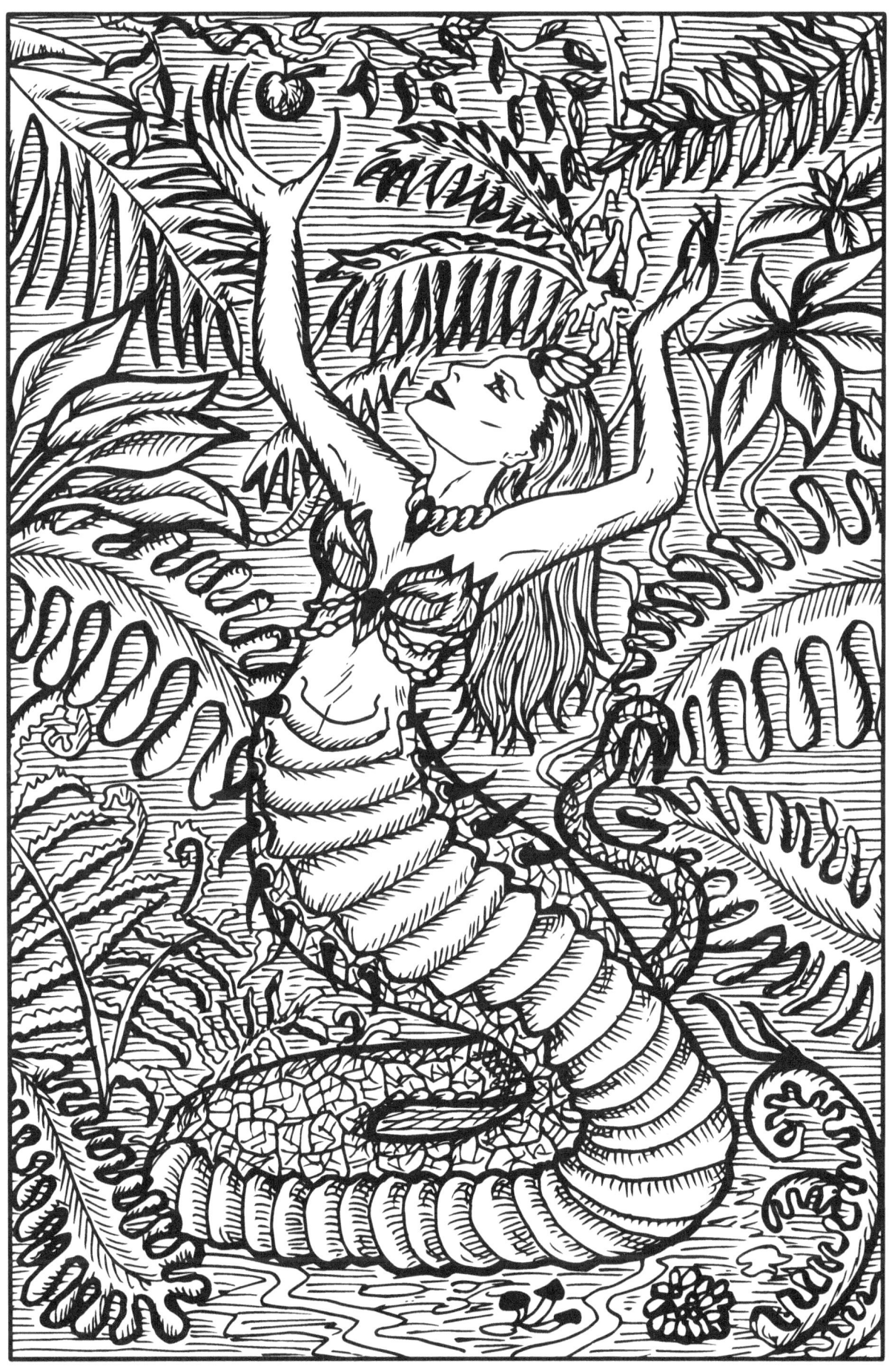

www.ingramcontent.com/pod-product-compliance
Lightning Source LLC
Chambersburg PA
CBHW080133240526
45468CB00009BA/2398